RECIPES FROM THE NIGHT KITCHEN

A Practical Guide

to

Spectacular

Soups,

Stews,

and Chilies

SALLY NIRENBERG

A FIRESIDE BOOK

Published by Simon & Schuster Inc. New York London Toronto Sydney Tokyo Singapore

Fireside
Simon & Schuster Building
Rockefeller Center
1230 Avenue of the Americas
New York, New York 10020

Illustrations by Janet Dennis
Manufactured in the United States of America

5 7 9 10 8 6 4

Library of Congress Cataloging in Publication Data

Nirenberg, Sally.
Recipes from the Night Kitchen : a practical guide to spectacular soups,
stews, and chilies / Sally Nirenberg.
p.   cm.
"A Fireside book."
1. Soups. 2. Stews. 3. Chili con carne. 4. From the Night
Kitchen (Restaurant) I. Title.
TX757.N57   1990
641.8′13—dc20   90-38393
                                            CIP
ISBN 0-671-68801-4

Acknowledgments

First and foremost, I want to thank my family. Both my parents and my brothers refused to cater to my many *quirks* about food while growing up; this *hardship* forced me to learn to cook and to be inventive.

Second, and perhaps of an equal but different importance, I want to thank all my loyal customers for being willing guinea pigs.

To Susan Orlean, for listening to me agonize over the writing process and for putting out many internal fires along the way.

To Danielle Abrams, Mary Burnham, Andre Clarke, Anna Gonzales, and Laura Putney, for running the store while I sat in front of my computer. Without them, I would never have been able to get out of the kitchen.

To my patient and wonderful friends for offering recipes, suggestions, criticisms, open ears, and, especially, open mouths: Eric Behr, Leah Bird, Toni Bowerman, Sharon Briggs, Mark Butler, Charles Cody, Sarah Conover, Bob Cowden, Cathy Dinardo, Emily Friedan, Judy and Mark Hershey, Gary Hoff, Joshua Jaffe, Anna Krantz, Carol Lesser, Donna Levin, Jack Levin, Marjorie Lyon, Julie Merberg, Sydny Miner, Gary Monzon, Darel Moss, Nancy Olin, Russ Robinson, Mark Sampson, John and Susan Schaub, Lizzy Shaw, Peter Sistrom, Jan and Bruce Spitz, Steve Steinberg, Cynthia Stuart, Peter Wheeler.

For Alice, who hated to cook, and for Sam,
who loved to eat.
And for Michael, who in his own way inspired
me.

Contents

SALLY NIRENBERG

Introductory
Notes

On November 19, 1982, I opened From the Night Kitchen at 24 Harvard Street in Brookline, Massachusetts. I had spent every penny that I owned, and some pennies of both my family and friends. I had wanted to own my own business for years, and after thinking long and hard about the effects of not doing what it was I really wanted to do, I decided to take a chance.

As unbelievable as it seems now (actually, things were a lot easier even as recently as then), I did not have a particularly clear idea of how to have what I wanted; I knew that I wanted to sell interesting and unusual foods and that I wanted to create an atmosphere where people felt comfortable. I did not think that I would be a cook. Like everyone else, I think I had the idea that I would sit around all day drinking wonderful, strong coffee and talking to interesting people.

It was not meant to be.

My original store was a cross between a café and a gourmet food shop. Meg and Peter Strattner, woodworkers I knew from a previous job, made me four dining tables, two display, and two worktables. They also made shelves for the walls, and cutting boards. I searched antique and thrift stores for old bentwood chairs; I bought two old eight-foot benches from a courtroom; I packed up all the pots and pans that I personally owned; I argued with the health department, hassled with the building department. I negotiated a lease, ordered catalogues, equipment, and merchandise. I hired electricians, plumbers, and painters and somehow I ended up with a store.

As the equipment and merchandise arrived, my friend John Schaub and I spent many long nights unpacking, pricing, and rearranging (it seemed that all we ever ate then was pizza). While I really did not know what I was doing and did not even know whom to ask for help (actually I didn't know that I didn't know), I had a strong sense of what I wanted the store to be: I only ordered the kind of cheeses that I liked, only the kind of crackers, oils, jams, spices, and teas that I had both tasted and appreciated. It was not egotism; I simply wanted to be sure that what I was selling was really special and that I could, in fact, sell it.

The day finally arrived for the doors to open; I spent the night before cooking. At home. I made onion soup with cream and carrot soup with fennel; three or four salads, including tarragon chicken, tuna with dill, potato salad, and probably something a bit more exotic (which has since been dropped from my repertoire); brownies and, of course, the obligatory chocolate chip cookies. I hung quilts that I had made in my more solitary years. I bought the wonderful, strong coffee of my fantasy, fresh, exotic bread, and several bouquets of fresh tulips. My friend Peter Wheeler, who eventually designed Brookline Place, came by with a big bouquet of roses just as I was about to open the doors, and rearranged everything that I had set up for display (I had to admit that his version looked better).

And then I really got to work.

It would be a lie to say that it was an immediate success; it was slow and frustrating. It was also fun and very exciting. I learned what people wanted and they learned to trust me and to take risks.

Eventually, I bade a sad farewell to all the strange and exotic goods; "gourmet" products were just emerging into the mainstream and I offered little that you couldn't get in the supermarket for a better price.

I was, at the same time, doing a phenomenal lunch business. I had added six sets of booths from an old diner (each complete with bubblegum under the tabletop), four more tables, and sixteen more chairs. I was constantly poaching huge bags of chicken, making chicken salad at all hours of night and day. I was preparing large batches of tuna salad, potato salad, pasta salad. But what I was really spending time on was soup.

By this time I had lots of helpers from Brookline High School. They would put on swim goggles and get to work on fifty-pound bags of Spanish onions: one person would peel, the other chop. I was having a blast; every day we would make several different soups, making old standbys like Minestrone (John and I called it "Liquid Gold," because it sold so well) and more exotic and unusual soups, with herbs that many customers had never heard of and often could not pronounce.

At first, people were very cautious and tried to stick to what they knew, but eventually they came around and seemed willing to try, literally, anything we served. I felt like all I ever did was make soup, but I had also found my niche.

I absolutely loved it; what was wonderful about making soup was that it encompassed every part of a meal and every season. I was making huge batches of Gazpacho in the summer the same way that I had been making huge batches of Minestrone in the winter. I was making soups for first courses, soups for main courses, soups for dessert. Hot soups, cold soups. The ability to experiment was endless. We could try anything; soups that were meant to be served hot were being served cold, soups that were meant to be served cold, hot. Friends and relatives offered recipes; dining out had become fieldwork.

Not being a perfectionist, I loved the flexibility of soup making. It didn't matter if you added too much stock—you could just cook it longer. It didn't matter if, when a recipe called for onions, you substituted leeks. What had originally been Curried Cream of Zucchini later became Curried Cream of Carrot and Curried Cream of Cauliflower. Soup making provided a great way to be creative and perhaps, most important, as long as the vegetables and the herbs were fresh and attention was paid you could really do no wrong.

Eventually, I felt that having a restaurant-café was not what I really wanted; I wanted to be in the kitchen as much as possible. While I loved the instant feedback, the demands of running a restaurant were taking me away from the kitchen and splitting me in ways that I did not want to be split. While I was debating the pros and cons of renewing my lease versus going into the wholesale soup business versus opening up a big restaurant (which would have driven me really crazy) versus sitting on the beach and reading magazines, in walked the developers of Brookline Place, a charming restoration of some old buildings, with a proposal that I open up a shop in one of their recently redeveloped buildings (just two blocks away).

The proposed store would, of course, be new, which in itself was appealing, and it would be designed to my specifications, because it was in a preconstruction state. It offered the possibility of starting over and yet staying where I was. It offered the possibility that I could put into use everything that I had learned over the past five years. It seemed that I could have my cake and eat it too.

After five years, the lease at my original store ran out and I did not renew it. Instead, I sold all the tables and chairs, all the booths. Once again, I argued with the health department, hassled with the building department, and negotiated a lease. I ordered catalogues, equipment, and merchandise. I hired electricians, plumbers, and painters, and this time, I opened a store for take-out only. After all, I wasn't spending my days sitting around drinking wonderful, strong coffee and talking to interesting people.

ON INGREDIENTS AND AMOUNTS

When I first envisioned this book, I thought back on all my years of making soup for my shop: We made massive amounts of soup in very few steps. All my store recipes use whole amounts of unpeeled ingredients like whole broccoli heads, cans of whole tomatoes, unpeeled whole potatoes (I do, however, peel carrots unless they are *very* clean, in which case, I scrub them). I hated to have little bits of things filling the refrigerator or, for that matter, the sink.

It was with these methods in mind that I wrote this book. In the recipes that follow, I rarely specify cups, preferrring to call for whole potatoes, whole carrots, whole onions. I generally use red potatoes which I do not peel: I like the flecks of color. I do not peel or seed tomatoes: I like the texture. Unless otherwise specified, all the soups are cooked uncovered; it concentrates the flavors.

My goal is for you to do the same and to feel the freedom to adjust accordingly. I do not want you to get caught up in precision; making soup calls for, no, it demands, flexibility. If you find that a soup is too thick because the broccoli head is larger than expected, simply add more stock or cream.

If this is too general and you want more explicit guidelines, here are some *general* equivalents:

Asparagus—1 pound trimmed and peeled = 3–3½ cups trimmed, peeled, and chopped

Broccoli—1 average head = 1½–1¾ pounds = 4½–5 cups chopped

Broccoli rabe—1 pound = 4 cups chopped

Butternut squash—1 large = 2–2½ pounds = 5 cups chopped

Carrots—1 medium = ⅙ pound = ¾ cup

Cauliflower—1 medium head = 2–2½ pounds = 5–6 cups chopped

Celeriac—1 large = 1 pound = 4–4½ cups

Celery—1 bunch = 12–14 stalks = 1¾–2 pounds

Corn—1 medium ear = ½ pound

Cucumber—1 medium = ½ pound

Eggplant—1 medium = 1–1½ pounds = 6 cups

Kale—1 pound = 5–7 cups chopped

Leeks—1 average bunch = 4–5 leeks = 2 pounds untrimmed

Mushrooms—1 pound = 6–7 cups trimmed and sliced

Parsnips—1 medium = ⅕ pound = ½–¾ cup

Peppers—1 medium = ⅓ pound
Potatoes—1 medium or 4 small = ½ pound = 2 cups diced
Pumpkin—1 medium = 5 pounds
Spanish onion—1 large = ¾ pound = 1½–2 cups
Spinach—1 pound = 8–9 cups chopped
Sweet potatoes—1 medium = ½–¾ pound = 2–2½ cups diced
Summer squash—1 medium = ½ pound = 1½–2 cups diced
Tomatoes—1 medium = ⅓ pound
Turnips—1 pound = 4 cups chopped
Watercress—1 pound = 3½ cups chopped
Zucchini—1 medium = ½ pound = 1¾ cups sliced

ESSENTIAL INGREDIENTS

There are a few ingredients that are essential to soup making. If you have these on hand, you can always make some kind of soup.

IN THE PANTRY

CANNED:
Artichoke bottoms, packed in
   water
Artichoke hearts, packed in
   water
Black turtle beans
Corn kernels
Kidney beans, dark red
Tomatoes, crushed
Tomatoes, whole peeled Ital-
   ian plum
Unsweetened pumpkin puree
White cannellini beans
DRY GOODS:
Black-eyed peas
Black turtle beans
Lentils
Navy beans
Split peas
White cannellini beans
Sun-dried tomatoes
Bouillon base and/or cubes:
   vegetable, chicken, and
   beef
Brown rice
Orzo
Pasta, various shapes and
   sizes
White rice
Brown sugar; white sugar
Unsweetened cocoa
All-purpose white flour,
   bleached or unbleached
Oils: olive, safflower, canola
Vinegar: red wine, balsamic

IN THE REFRIGERATOR

Dijon mustard
Margarine
Sun-dried tomatoes, packed
    in oil

ALCOHOL

Cognac
Dry red wine
Dry Sherry
Dry white wine
Frangelico
Harpoon ale; beer
Triple Sec or other orange li-
    queur

FRUITS AND VEGETABLES

Carrots
Celery
Garlic
Lemons
Limes
Potatoes
Red onions
Scallions
Shallots
Spanish onions
Tomatoes

FREEZER

Bacon
Cut-up chicken
Unsalted butter

ON HERBS AND SPICES

The quality of the herbs and spices you use, whether dried or fresh, is absolutely critical to successful soup making. I usually use dried herbs; they stand up better to long cooking. In some recipes, however, I have noted the amount of fresh herbs that may be substituted.

I've found that the best dried herbs and spices are sold by Dean and DeLuca in New York City.* Their spices are available in many specialty stores around the country and also by mail order. While they appear to be more expensive than those found in supermarkets, ounce for ounce, they are actually less expensive.

*Dean and DeLuca, 560 Broadway, New York, NY 10012. Telephone 1 (800) 221-7714

The Dean and DeLuca line is packed in tins, which I prefer. Spices stored in glass or plastic containers should be stored out of direct sunlight.

Buy small amounts. Both herbs and ground spices decrease in potency with time, and with exposure to the air and sunlight.

DRIED HERBS AND SPICES

Basil

Bay leaves

Caraway seeds

Cayenne

Chili powder

Cinnamon

Cumin

Curry powder*

French tarragon

Greek oregano

Hungarian paprika

Marjoram

Nutmeg

Red pepper flakes

Rosemary

Sage

Thyme

FRESH HERBS

Most grocery and vegetable stores now carry a full array of fresh herbs, even in the winter. I use curly parsley and dill the most extensively and would never consider using either in dried form.

Cilantro must be used fresh. The dried form is called coriander and the taste is *very* different. If you cannot find fresh cilantro, skip any recipe calling for it.

---

*A note about curry powder: Purists insist that you grind your own curry powder; I have tried to do this and I must admit that I have not been able to make one that I like as well as the Dean and DeLuca blend. I think that it is important not to get too carried away—leave some things to the experts.

ON STOCKS AND BROTHS

It is, perhaps, heresy to say so, but I think that the importance of making your own stock has been greatly overrated.

The culinary world's insistence on making homemade stock has, I think, prevented many otherwise gifted would-be soup makers from making soup. There are many stocks, broths, and soup bases on the market that are excellent. Some have MSG, some do not. Some have salt, some do not. Choosing which one is right for you is really a matter of personal taste. I will not intentionally eat anything with MSG in it, and I know that a lot of people are allergic to it; it is something to watch out for. Many health-food stores carry chicken and vegetable bases that are made without stabilizers or enhancers of any kind.

While clear and brothlike soups are somewhat better when made with homemade stocks, I have found that most of the soups that I make rely less on the base and more on the flavoring of the main ingredient and/or herb.

Do try making your own stock; there is something very satisfying about the process and the results are, of course, worth the work—but only *if* you think that it is important, *if* you enjoy making it, and *if* you have the time.

The recipe for Matzoh Ball Soup (page 92) makes an excellent chicken stock and the recipe for Onion Soup (page 53) makes an excellent vegetable stock. If you're looking for a good beef stock, I recommend the recipes in Julia Child's *The Way to Cook* (Knopf, 1989) or Bernard Clayton's *The Complete Book of Soups and Stews* (Fireside, 1984).

ON EQUIPMENT

Before I opened up my shop on Harvard Street I worked at a store called Crate and Barrel which sold, among other things, great housewares and cooking equipment. When I worked there I was absolutely unable to sell Cuisinarts or any other machines; I was convinced that the joy of cooking came from the hands-on process. After having chopped literally tons of vegetables and having whipped dozens and dozens of eggs by hand, I have changed my tune. While I still cherish my knives, I also cherish my Cuisinart.

Making soup can be as complicated or as simple as you wish; most soups can be made with a knife and a cutting board. A food mill will puree a soup very well if you don't have a food processor or blender. However, should you want or require ease, I have included my preferences and recommendations. In many cases, I recommend particular brands and name them here, because time and experience have taught me that while it often makes sense to buy the most expensive piece, it often does not. I have bought equipment of the most utilitarian sort and been happy, and I have bought equipment just to have something beautiful to look at. The first is a matter of experience, the second, taste. My hope is that this list will prevent you from having to replace pieces you buy now with different pieces later.

Heavy-bottomed 4-quart and 6-quart stockpots (such as Calphalon or All Clad)

Food processor (I use a Cuisinart)

Blender (I use an Oster)

Mouli food mill

Strainer or colander

Assorted ladles: 4-ounce, 6-ounce

Assorted wooden spoons

Good knives (my favorite brands are Victorinox and Sabatier)

Vegetable peeler (the best I've found is Westmark)

Pepper mill

Corkscrew

Measuring cups and spoons

Whisks

Graters

RECIPES
FROM
THE
NIGHT
KITCHEN

Vegetable Soups

Vegetable soups are the easiest, most varied, and most versatile soups of all. Most can be made from start to finish in less than an hour and almost all lend themselves to creative substitutions. With the exception of tomatoes, corn, and artichokes, always use fresh vegetables, but feel free to experiment.

★ Try broccoli instead of zucchini in Zucchini Potato.
★ Substitute cauliflower for broccoli in Broccoli with Dill.
★ Use yogurt or buttermilk instead of heavy or sour cream in the cream soups.
★ Adjust the liquid: more or less will thin or thicken a soup.

I have made recommendations for substituting and for chilling, but once again, use your imagination.

Artichoke with Lemon

When I first opened From the Night Kitchen I was not very good at ordering merchandise, nor was I organized enough to send anything back. A case of artichoke bottoms arrived and out of necessity this soup was born.

Do not use an aluminum pot to make this soup.

¼ cup unsalted butter
¼ cup all-purpose white flour
6 cloves garlic, pressed or finely chopped
Juice of 1 lemon
6 cups chicken broth
2 14-ounce cans artichoke bottoms packed in water, rinsed and drained
Freshly ground black pepper

1. Melt butter over low heat in a heavy-bottomed saucepan or stockpot. Whisk in flour very slowly.

2. Gradually add garlic, lemon juice, chicken broth, and artichoke bottoms and bring to a boil. Reduce heat to low and simmer for 25 to 35 minutes.

3. Remove solids and place in a food processor or blender. Process until smooth, gradually adding remaining broth. Add pepper and serve.

VARIATIONS:

Cream of Artichoke: Decrease chicken broth by ½ cup and add ½ cup heavy or light cream to pureed soup.
Substitute two 14-ounce cans artichoke hearts, packed in water, for the artichoke bottoms.

Asparagus with Tarragon

1 tablespoon unsalted butter, olive or canola oil
1 Spanish onion, coarsely chopped
2 cloves garlic, pressed or finely chopped
1 pound fresh asparagus
4–5 cups chicken stock
½ teaspoon dried tarragon, or 1½ teaspoons chopped fresh
½ teaspoon Dijon mustard
¼ teaspoon ground nutmeg

1.   Melt butter or oil over low heat in a 3-quart soup pot. Add onion and garlic and cook, covered, until golden, 10 to 15 minutes.

2.   Break off woody ends of asparagus and discard. (I suggest that you use your hands rather than a knife; the ends will break off at the point where the stalk is tender.) Peel the asparagus stalks with a potato peeler; chop off tips and set aside. Coarsely chop remaining asparagus and add to onion.

3.   Add chicken stock, tarragon, and Dijon mustard and bring to a boil. Reduce heat to low and simmer for 35 to 45 minutes.

4.   Remove solids and place in a food processor or blender. Process until smooth, gradually adding remaining broth.

5.   Strain the soup if you like. (Straining will get rid of the slight stringiness. This is a matter of taste.) Add nutmeg, and garnish each bowl with reserved asparagus tips.

VARIATIONS:

Cream of Asparagus: Decrease chicken broth by ½ cup and add ½ cup heavy cream after the soup has been pureed.
Chilled Asparagus: Double the amount of mustard and tarragon used and chill for 2 hours. Garnish just before serving.

Customers always know that spring has arrived when this soup shows up on the menu. Make the soup only when asparagus is fresh, from March through June, and use only straight, green, crisp stalks.

I HAVE THE
SIMPLEST OF
TASTES...
I AM ALWAYS
SATISFIED
WITH THE BEST.
Oscar Wilde

SALLY NIRENBERG
27

Broccoli with Dill

When I first started making soup, it never occurred to me to make broccoli soup, because I always thought of broccoli as a vegetable that children were forced to eat. My friend Carrie Scheer gave me this recipe and it is one of the most popular soups at my shop, summer and winter, hot or cold.

The real secret to making broccoli soup is not to overcook the broccoli. Do not add it until the stock has come to a full boil.

1 tablespoon unsalted butter, olive or canola oil
1 Spanish onion, coarsely chopped
1 stalk celery, chopped
1 small carrot, peeled and thinly sliced
5–6 cups chicken stock (depending on size of broccoli head)
1 head broccoli, woody stems discarded, florets chopped
Chopped fresh dill
Salt and pepper

1. Melt butter or oil over low heat in a 4-quart soup pot. Add onion, celery, and carrot and cook, covered, until vegetables are tender, 10 to 15 minutes.

2. Add chicken stock and bring to a boil. While broth is boiling, slowly add broccoli florets. Return to a boil briefly.

3. Reduce heat to medium and cook until broccoli is tender, 15 to 20 minutes.

4. Remove solids and place in a food processor or blender. Process until smooth, gradually adding remaining broth. Add more stock if soup is too thick.

5. Season with dill, salt and pepper to taste.

VARIATIONS:

Cream of Broccoli: Decrease chicken stock by ½ cup and add ½ cup heavy or light cream and ½ teaspoon ground nutmeg after the soup has been pureed.

For a cream soup lower in calories and cholesterol, substitute ½ cup nonfat yogurt or buttermilk for heavy or sour cream. Do not bring this version to a boil when reheating, or the soup will curdle.

Broccoli Cauliflower with Basil and Parmesan

This soup was developed after constant requests that I make a low-cholesterol soup that doesn't taste dull. It tastes wonderfully rich, and while it can be made with either cauliflower or broccoli alone, it is more interesting when both are used.

Make sure that you do not add the broccoli until the broth has come to a boil.

1 tablespoon olive or canola oil
1 Spanish onion, coarsely chopped
6 cups chicken stock
2 cups water
1 potato, unpeeled, diced (about 1 cup)
½ head broccoli, woody stems discarded, florets chopped
½ head cauliflower, cored and chopped
2 tablespoons dried basil, or ⅓ cup chopped fresh
⅓ cup grated Parmesan cheese

1.   Heat oil over low flame in a 4-quart pot. Add onion and cook, covered, until golden, 10 to 15 minutes.

2.   Add chicken stock, water, and potato and bring to a boil.

3.   Add broccoli, cauliflower, and basil. Return soup to a boil. Reduce heat to low and cook until broccoli is tender, about 15 minutes.

4.   Remove solids and place in a blender or food processor, gradually adding remaining broth and Parmesan. Do not puree; this soup should be chunky.

VARIATIONS:

Replace basil with ½ bunch fresh dill and Parmesan with ½ cup sour cream (for those not concerned with cholesterol).
Replace the Parmesan with low-fat or nonfat yogurt or buttermilk.

Broccoli Rabe and Orzo

1 tablespoon olive oil
1 Spanish onion, finely chopped
3 cloves garlic, pressed or finely chopped
1 pound broccoli rabe, woody stems discarded, leaves coarsely
    chopped and rinsed in very hot water
6 cups chicken stock
½ cup rice, orzo, or any very small pasta
Grated Parmesan cheese
Sour cream or crème fraîche

1.   Heat oil over low flame in a 3-quart pot. Add onion and garlic and cook, covered, until golden, 10 to 15 minutes.

2.   Add just-washed (but not dried) broccoli rabe, cover, and sauté/steam for 10 minutes.

3.   Add stock and bring to a boil. Add rice or orzo, reduce heat to medium-low, and simmer for 20 minutes. Serve immediately, topped with grated Parmesan and a dollop of sour cream or crème fraîche.

VARIATIONS:

Substitute spinach or romaine for the broccoli rabe.
Substitute crumbled Gorgonzola or blue cheese for the Parmesan.

Broccoli rabe, also called rapini or broccoli rape, is not actually broccoli, but another member of the cabbage family. It is a bitter green; the first time that I made this soup I oversalted it to compensate for that. Don't make the same mistake; the slight bitterness is wonderful. I've been known to eat this right out of the soup pot, when it's barely done, and right out of the refrigerator, when it's icy cold.

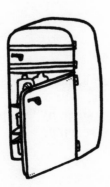

SALLY NIRENBERG

31

Broccoli Tomato with Parmesan and Oregano

The idea for this soup came from my friend John Schaub. I resisted and resisted, but when I finally made it, I was absolutely delighted.

1 tablespoon olive or canola oil
1 Spanish onion, coarsely chopped
3 cloves garlic, pressed or finely chopped
1 tablespoon dried Greek oregano, or 2 tablespoons chopped fresh
2 16-ounce cans Italian plum tomatoes, coarsely chopped
8 cups chicken stock
1 head broccoli, woody stems discarded, florets coarsely chopped
½ cup chopped fresh parsley
½ cup grated Parmesan cheese
Ricotta cheese

1.   Heat oil in a 3-quart soup pot over low flame. Add onion and garlic and cook, covered, until golden, 10 to 15 minutes.

2.   Add oregano, tomatoes and their juice, and chicken stock; bring to a boil.

3.   Add broccoli florets and parsley, reduce heat to low, and cook, partially covered, until broccoli is tender, about 25 minutes.

4.   Stir in Parmesan. Garnish each portion with a dollop of ricotta cheese before serving.

VARIATIONS:

Prior to adding broccoli, puree the soup. This gives it a completely different texture.
Decrease the chicken stock by ½ cup and add ½ cup heavy or light cream just before serving.

Butternut Squash and Tomato

1 tablespoon olive or canola oil
1 Spanish onion, finely chopped
2 garlic cloves, pressed or finely chopped
2 teaspoons chili powder
¼ teaspoon ground cumin
1 butternut squash (about 2–2½ pounds), peeled, seeded, and
    cubed (5 cups)
2 fresh tomatoes, diced
7 cups chicken or vegetable stock
Pinch sugar
½ cup chopped fresh parsley leaves
1 bay leaf
1 lime

Most winter squash soups are smooth purees. In this rendition, you partially puree and as a result you end up with a wholly different, but surprisingly wonderful, texture. Adjust the chili and the cumin to suit your desire for spiciness.

1.   Heat oil over low flame in a 3-quart pot. Add onion, garlic, chili powder, and cumin and cook, covered, until the onion has wilted, 10 to 15 minutes.

2.   Add squash, tomatoes, stock, sugar, parsley, and bay leaf and bring to a boil. Reduce heat to low and simmer, partially covered, until squash is tender, about 20 minutes.

3.   Remove bay leaf and discard. Remove half the solids and place in a food processor or blender. Process until smooth, gradually adding 1 cup broth; return to soup pot. Cook over low heat for 1 hour.

4.   Squeeze juice of lime over soup just prior to serving.

Butternut Squash with Apples and Almonds

My favorite soup, slightly spicy, slightly sweet and velvety, it tastes and feels like a cream soup without having any cream in it. When I first made it, I had been experimenting with soups all day long, bringing samples to my neighbors, Mark and Judy Hershey. After having had a bowl of split pea, a bowl of artichoke, and a bowl of asparagus (all made with cream), Mark had two bowls of this one. This did not stop him from asking for more on the following day.

1 tablespoon unsalted butter or olive oil
1 Spanish onion, coarsely chopped
1 butternut squash (about 2–2½ pounds) peeled, seeded, and chopped (5 cups)
1 Granny Smith apple, unpeeled, cored, and chopped
12 whole almonds
5 cups chicken stock
½ teaspoon dried marjoram, or 1½ teaspoons chopped fresh
½–1½ teaspoons curry powder
1 teaspoon brown sugar (optional)
½ cup dry white wine

1. Melt butter or oil over low heat in a heavy-bottomed saucepan or stockpot. Add onion and cook, covered, until golden, 10 to 15 minutes.

2. Add remaining ingredients and bring to a boil. Reduce heat to low and cook, covered, until squash is tender, about 20 minutes.

3. Remove solids and place in a food processor or blender. Process until smooth, gradually adding remaining broth.

VARIATIONS:

Substitute pistachio nuts, hazelnuts, pecans, or walnuts for the almonds.
Substitute an orange, peeled, seeded, and chopped, for the apple.

Butternut Squash with Garlic, Ginger, and Lime

1 tablespoon unsalted butter
1 Spanish onion, coarsely chopped
4 cloves garlic, pressed or finely chopped
1 tablespoon peeled, coarsely chopped fresh ginger
1 butternut squash (approximately 2–2½ pounds), peeled, seeded, and chopped (5 cups)
5 cups chicken stock
Pinch sugar
¼ cup fresh lime juice
Fresh lime slices

1.   Melt butter over low heat in a heavy-bottomed soup pot. Add onion, garlic, and ginger and cook, covered, for 15 to 20 minutes, stirring occasionally.

2.   Add butternut squash, chicken stock, and sugar and bring to a boil. Reduce heat to low and cook until squash is tender, 20 to 25 minutes.

3.   Remove solids and place in a food processor or blender. Process until smooth, gradually adding remaining broth and lime juice.

4.   Float slices of fresh lime on each serving.

The idea for this soup came from Dr. Paul Staulcup, a man so enamored of soup he often orders a quart for lunch. His suggestion proved that he was well worth listening to.

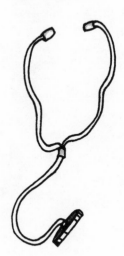

SALLY NIRENBERG

Cabbage with Bacon and Cream

This is a hearty, thick winter soup. Serve it with a very black rye bread and a salad of mixed greens.

¼ pound bacon, finely chopped
1 Spanish onion, finely chopped
2 carrots, peeled and coarsely chopped
¼ cup all-purpose white flour
8 cups chicken stock
2 medium potatoes (about ¾–1 pound), unpeeled, diced (about 3 cups)
1 very small green cabbage (about 1½ pounds), shredded
1 tablespoon caraway seeds
½ teaspoon black pepper
1–1½ cups heavy cream

1.   Cook bacon over medium heat in a 4-quart pot until rendered of all fat. Discard all fat except that needed to sauté the onion, about 2 tablespoons. Sauté onion and carrots in the fat until vegetables are tender, 10 to 15 minutes.

2.   Sprinkle flour on vegetables, while stirring with a spoon. Slowly add stock, stirring constantly, and bring to a boil.

3.   Reduce heat to low and add potatoes, cabbage, caraway seeds, and pepper and cook for 1 hour. Do not let it boil again.

4.   Gradually stir in heavy cream and cook over very low heat for 20 minutes. Serve immediately.

Carrot with Fennel

1 tablespoon olive or canola oil
1 Spanish onion, coarsely chopped
1½–2 pounds carrots, peeled and sliced
8 cups chicken or vegetable stock
1 teaspoon dried fennel seed

1.   Heat oil over low flame in a 3-quart soup pot. Add onion and carrots and cook, covered, until vegetables are tender, 15 to 20 minutes.

2.   Add stock and fennel and bring to a boil. Reduce heat to low and simmer for 20 minutes.

3.   Remove solids and place in a food processor or blender. Process until smooth, gradually adding remaining broth.

This is one of the first soups that I served at the Harvard Street store; I have a special affection for it. It is an unusual and subtle combination of flavors, and it is a rare guest that can guess the ingredients of this beautifully colored soup.

SALLY NIRENBERG

37

Carrot with Ginger Cream

This soup cemented my friendship with Susan Orlean. Before we became friends, she used to come in all the time begging me for carrot soup; I was forced to give her the recipe. This soup has a nice bite to it but you wouldn't describe it as spicy. It is perfect to serve to both children and adults. Try it for a winter lunch with grilled cheese and tomato sandwiches and, for the adults, a well-chilled Chardonnay. In the summer, try it chilled, accompanied by just the Chardonnay.

1 tablespoon unsalted butter
1 medium Spanish onion, coarsely chopped
2 pounds carrots, peeled and sliced
Pinch ground cinnamon
8 cups chicken stock
2 teaspoons peeled, coarsely chopped fresh ginger
½ cup heavy cream

1.   Melt butter over low heat in a heavy-bottomed saucepan or stockpot. Add onion and carrots and cook, covered, until vegetables are tender, 15 to 20 minutes.

2.   Add cinnamon, chicken stock, and ginger and bring to a boil. Reduce heat to low and cook for 30 minutes.

3.   Remove solids and place in a food processor or blender. Process until completely smooth, gradually adding remaining broth and heavy cream.

VARIATIONS:

   To reduce cholesterol, substitute olive or canola oil for the butter and omit the cream.
   Substitute apple juice or buttermilk for the cream.

Cauliflower with Cheddar

2 tablespoons unsalted butter
1 large Spanish onion, coarsely chopped
½ teaspoon white sugar
1 head cauliflower, core removed, florets coarsely chopped
6 cups chicken stock
½–¾ cup grated extra-sharp Cheddar cheese
Freshly ground black pepper
Chopped fresh dill
Finely chopped scallions (white and green parts)

1. Melt butter over medium heat in a heavy-bottomed saucepan or stockpot. Add onion and sugar and cook, uncovered, until onion has caramelized, about 20 minutes. Onion should be soft and browned but not burnt.

2. Add cauliflower and chicken stock and bring to a boil. Reduce heat to low and cook until cauliflower is tender, about 25 minutes.

3. Remove solids and place in a food processor or blender. Process until smooth, gradually adding cheese, pepper, and remaining broth.

4. Garnish each serving with chopped dill and scallions.

On Thanksgiving morning several years ago, my friend Mark Butler invited me to his house for breakfast. He offered me an omelet (which I hate), filled with Cheddar cheese and cauliflower (which I almost hate). While I was tempted to decline, somehow I just couldn't: the combination of someone actually cooking for me and Mark's enthusiasm forced me to try what turned out to be one of my very favorite meals. I decided to see if this combination could do for soup what it did for omelets.

Spicy Cauliflower

This soup is somewhat reminiscent of those found in Indian restaurants. Spice it up by using the larger amount of curry.

1 tablespoon olive or canola oil
1 large Spanish onion, coarsely chopped
2 garlic cloves, pressed or finely chopped
½–1½ teaspoons curry powder
½ teaspoon Dijon mustard
6 cups chicken stock
1 large red new potato, chopped (about 1–1½ cups)
1 head cauliflower, cored and coarsely chopped
½ teaspoon dried thyme
½ teaspoon ground nutmeg
1 cup heavy cream
Sour cream
Chopped fresh cilantro leaves

1.   Heat oil over low flame in a heavy-bottomed pot. Add onion, garlic, and curry and cook, covered, until onion has wilted, 10 to 15 minutes.

2.   Add mustard, chicken stock, and potato and bring to a boil.

3.   Reduce heat to low and add cauliflower, thyme, and nutmeg. Cook until cauliflower is tender, 25 to 30 minutes.

4.   Remove solids and place in a food processor or blender. Process until completely smooth, gradually adding remaining broth and heavy cream.

5.   Serve each portion with a dollop of sour cream and cilantro.

VARIATION:

Omit heavy cream, or substitute it with buttermilk or low-fat yogurt.

Celeriac and Potato

1 leek, greens included
1 tablespoon unsalted butter
1 clove garlic, pressed or finely chopped
1 pound celeriac (celery root), peeled and diced
½ pound potatoes, unpeeled, diced (about 2 cups)
7–8 cups chicken or vegetable stock
½ cup heavy cream.
Finely chopped scallions (green and white parts)
Chopped fresh tarragon leaves

This soup is a combination of vichyssoise and cream of celery— really the best of both, combining the silky texture of vichyssoise with the taste of celery root.

1. Cut off root end and 3 inches of green part of leek and discard. Quarter leek lengthwise and thinly slice. Soak in several changes of water, being careful to get rid of all the sand.

2. Melt butter over low heat in a heavy-bottomed saucepan or stockpot. Add leek and garlic and cook, covered, until leek has wilted, 10 to 15 minutes.

3. Add celeriac, potatoes, and stock and bring to a boil. Let boil for 5 minutes. Reduce heat to medium and cook until potato and celeriac are tender, 20 to 35 minutes.

4. Remove solids and place in a food processor or blender. Process until completely smooth, gradually adding remaining broth and heavy cream.

5. Garnish each serving with chopped scallions and tarragon leaves.

Cream of Celery

My clearest memory of being sick as a child is of my mother bringing me Cream of Celery soup, Ritz crackers, *Seventeen* and *Glamour* magazines, and Colorforms. While I have outgrown everything else, I still think of Cream of Celery as comforting and healing.

1 tablespoon unsalted butter
1 large shallot, coarsely chopped
6 scallions, including greens, thinly sliced
1 bunch celery, including heart and leaves, peeled and thinly sliced
6 cups chicken or vegetable broth
1 large Idaho potato, unpeeled, cubed
1 teaspoon dried rosemary, or 1 tablespoon chopped fresh
½ teaspoon ground nutmeg
½ cup heavy or light cream

1.   Melt butter over low heat in a heavy-bottomed saucepan or stockpot. Add shallot, scallions, and celery and cook, covered, until vegetables have wilted, 10 to 15 minutes.

2.   Add broth, potato, and rosemary and bring to a boil. Reduce heat to low and simmer until celery and potato are tender, about 25 minutes.

3.   Remove solids and place in a food processor or blender. Process until completely smooth, gradually adding remaining broth, nutmeg, and cream.

VARIATION:

For those watching their cholesterol, simply omit the cream.

MODERATION IS A VASTLY OVERRATED VIRTUE.
Bette Davis in the Corn is Green

Cilantro-Ginger with Cream

1 tablespoon unsalted butter
1 Spanish onion, coarsely chopped
1 stalk celery, peeled and coarsely chopped
2–3 tablespoons fresh gingerroot, peeled and sliced into coins
2–3 cloves garlic, sliced
6 cups chicken stock
½ cup chopped fresh cilantro leaves
1 cup heavy cream.

1.   Melt butter over low heat in a heavy-bottomed saucepan or stockpot. Add onion, celery, ginger, and garlic and cook, covered, until vegetables have wilted, about 20 minutes.

2.   Add chicken stock and bring to a boil.

3.   Remove solids and place in a food processor or blender with chopped cilantro. Process until smooth, gradually adding heavy cream.

4.   Return puree to soup and cook, uncovered, over very low heat for 30 minutes, stirring frequently. Be very careful not to let it boil.

Cilantro is a flavor that people either adore or abhor. This soup is rich, velvety, and delicious, a wonderful way to introduce the distinctive flavor of cilantro. Serve it in the spring with grilled swordfish or chicken.

Never ever consider using anything other than fresh cilantro; if you can't find it, don't make this soup.

1 tablespoon ...
Scrub onion, carrots, chopped
1 inch celery, peeled or rediced or sliced
2-3 tablespoons lard, undissolved bean or cracked into chunks
1-2 ... sauce
3 cups chicken stock
... cup chopped fresh cilantro leaves
1 cup bean sprouts

1. Heat butter or oil in a heavy ... pan over moderate heat. Add the ... onion, carrot, and celery and cook until ... brown and softened, about ...

2. ... stock ... add the ...

3. Remove ... and set aside ... season to taste with additional salt. Ladle the soup into ... salad and ... croutons.

4. Blend together ... into the ... and ...

Corn with Basil

1 tablespoon olive or canola oil
1 small onion, coarsely chopped
1 garlic clove, pressed or finely chopped
6 large ears of corn, kernels scraped or cut off (approximately 4
    cups), or 2 17-ounce cans corn
5 cups chicken or vegetable stock
2–3 teaspoons dried basil, or 3 tablespoons chopped fresh
Pinch sugar
Fresh basil leaves
Chopped red pepper

1.   Heat oil over low flame in a 3-quart pot. Add onion and garlic and cook, covered, until golden, 10 to 15 minutes.

2.   Raise heat to medium; add corn, stock, basil, and sugar; and cook, partially covered, for 25 minutes.

3.   Transfer half the solids to a food processor or blender and puree. Return puree to soup, stir, and serve immediately.

4.   Garnish each portion with fresh basil leaves and chopped red pepper.

VARIATION:

Substitute fresh cilantro for the basil and add 1 chopped red pepper when you add the corn.

My father is *very* serious about his low-cholesterol diet, and eating with him, or at least cooking for him, can be boring.

I was at my father's with my younger brother, Peter, who is very serious about eating, and watching his cholesterol simply does not come into consideration. Creating a soup to satisfy both of them was a challenge. This was my solution, and ever since they've both been begging for more. Of course, I never let Peter know how virtuous he's being when he eats this soup.

Five Pepper

As a rule, I do not like the taste or the texture of cooked peppers, so when Michelle Kelley suggested making this soup, I was adamantly opposed. I had never had and had never even heard of a sweet pepper soup that I liked. This is the exception to the rule.

1 tablespoon unsalted butter
1 Spanish onion, coarsely chopped
2 red peppers, cored and cut into big strips
2 green peppers, cored and cut into big strips
2 yellow peppers, cored and cut into big strips
6 cups vegetable or chicken stock
½ teaspoon Hungarian paprika
1–2 teaspoons Dijon mustard
1 cup sour cream
¼ cup chopped fresh dill
Lots of freshly ground pepper

1.   Melt butter over medium heat in a heavy-bottomed saucepan or stockpot. Add onion and peppers and cook, covered, until the peppers have somewhat softened, 10 to 15 minutes.

2.   Add stock, paprika, and mustard and bring to a boil.

3.   Remove peppers from soup pot and transfer them to the bowl of a food processor fitted with a steel blade. Pulse the peppers until they are bite size. Return to soup pot and simmer for 10 minutes.

4.   Gently add sour cream, chopped dill, and ground pepper, stirring all the time.

VARIATIONS:

Use peppers of one color.
Substitute 2 chopped tomatoes for the 2 red peppers.
Substitute fresh cilantro for the dill.

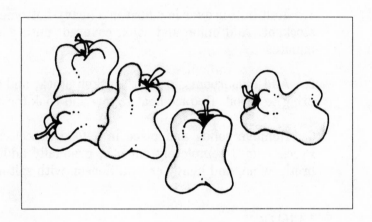

Cream of Mushroom

1 tablespoon unsalted butter
1 Spanish onion, coarsely chopped or sliced
¾ pound fresh mushrooms, coarsely chopped, stems included
1 potato, unpeeled, diced (about 1 cup)
4 cups chicken stock
1 teaspoon dried rosemary, or 3 teaspoons chopped fresh
¼ cup dry red wine
½ cup heavy cream
Salt and pepper to taste

1.   Melt butter over low heat in a heavy-bottomed saucepan or stockpot. Add onion and cook, covered, until golden, 10 to 15 minutes.

2.   Add mushrooms, potato, chicken stock, and rosemary and bring to a boil. Reduce heat to low and cook for 30 minutes.

3.   Remove solids and place in a food processor or blender. Process until completely smooth, gradually adding remaining broth, wine, and heavy cream. Season with salt and pepper.

VARIATION:

For a slightly sweeter soup, substitute sherry for the red wine.

Hunter's Soup

1 tablespoon unsalted butter
1 Spanish onion, finely chopped
1 shallot, finely chopped
2 cloves garlic, pressed or finely chopped
1 stalk celery, thinly sliced
1 carrot, peeled, halved lengthwise, and thinly sliced
6 cups chicken or beef stock
1 pound mushrooms, cut into eighths
1 16-ounce can whole tomatoes, drained and coarsely chopped
1 cup dry red or white wine
2 tablespoons chopped fresh parsley
½ teaspoon dried rosemary, or 1½ teaspoons chopped fresh
½ teaspoon dried thyme, or 1½ teaspoons chopped fresh

1.   Melt butter over medium heat in a heavy-bottomed saucepan or stockpot. Add onion, shallot, garlic, celery, and carrot and cook, covered, until vegetables are tender, about 25 minutes, stirring occasionally.

2.   Add stock, mushrooms, tomatoes and their juice, wine, and herbs. Simmer for 2 hours, uncovered, or until soup has reduced by one quarter.

VARIATION:

To make a delicious sauce for pasta, start with 4 cups stock instead of 6. You should get 7–8 cups sauce.

In 1988 Regina Schrambling wrote a piece for the *New York Times* called "Eating to Hunt"—this is a variation of her Semi-Classic Hunter Sauce. As soon as I saw the recipe I knew that it would make a great soup, and I was right.

Bittersweet Chocolate Moons

1/2 cup butter (or margarine)
3/4 cup walnuts
1/3 cup white sugar
1/2 cup unsweetened cocoa
1 cup white flour
1/4 teaspoon vanilla extract

put all ingredients in cuisinart
and blend until a ball forms.

chill one hour.

form into 12 balls and shape
into moons (crescent)

bake at 300 on an ungreased
cookie sheet for 15-20
minutes.

Mushroom, Leek, and Barley

1 bunch leeks (about 1 pound, or 3 large)
1 tablespoon olive or canola oil
4 cloves garlic, pressed or finely chopped
1 carrot, peeled, halved lengthwise, and sliced
8–10 cups beef or chicken stock
2 teaspoons dried thyme, or 2 tablespoons chopped fresh
½ cup barley
1½ cups dry red wine
¾–1 pound mushrooms, sliced

This is a hearty, rich soup that can be served as a meal in itself. Just add cheese; dark, crusty bread; and for dessert, something sinful.

1.   Cut off root end and 3 inches of green part of leeks and discard. Quarter leeks lengthwise and thinly slice. Soak them in several changes of water, being careful to get rid of all the sand.

2.   Heat oil over low flame in a heavy-bottomed pot. Add leeks and garlic and cook, covered, until leeks have wilted, about 20 minutes.

3.   Add remaining ingredients and bring to a boil. Reduce heat to low and cook, partially covered, for 3 to 4 hours. (You may need to add additional stock at this point, depending on how thick or thin you want the soup to be.)

VARIATIONS:

Substitute wild rice for the barley.
Add ¼ cup corn, tomatoes, or spinach when you add the mushrooms.

SALLY NIRENBERG

Mushroom with Frangelico

Last Christmas I received a bottle of Frangelico from my friend Robert Balestieri, who owns Village Fruit in Brookline. I had never tasted it before and thought it was the most wonderful thing I had ever tasted. Having exhausted the nighttime drink possibilities, I looked for ways to use it in cooking. Heating it wasn't successful, but adding it as a finish creates an incredibly subtle and smooth flavor. This velvety soup is best eaten immediately after it is made.

5 tablespoons unsalted butter
5 tablespoons all-purpose white flour
4–5 cups chicken stock
1 pound mushrooms, stems trimmed, thinly sliced
⅓ cup Frangelico or other hazelnut liqueur

1.   Melt butter over very low heat in a heavy-bottomed sauce-pan or stockpot; when butter has melted, slowly whisk in flour until mixture resembles mashed potatoes. Continue whisking while adding chicken stock and until all stock is incorporated and mixture is smooth.

2.   Add mushrooms and cook, uncovered, over low heat for 1 hour, stirring occasionally. Do not shorten the cooking time or you will lose the depth of flavor that makes this soup so special.

3.   Remove half the solids and place in a food processor or blender. Process until smooth, gradually adding 1 cup broth. Return to remaining soup and add the Frangelico.

Onion

¼ cup unsalted butter
3 large Spanish onions, finely sliced or chopped (about 6–7 cups)
3 cloves garlic, pressed or finely chopped
½ teaspoon white sugar
7 cups beef or chicken stock
1 cup dry red wine
1 teaspoon dried thyme, or 1 tablespoon chopped fresh
¼ cup Cognac

The truth is that French Onion Soup is hard to improve upon. This is a slight departure from the classic recipe but, I think, a nice one. This also makes a wonderfully rich stock to use in other soups.

1. Melt butter over low to medium heat in a heavy-bottomed soup pot. Add onions and cook, covered, over low heat for 45 minutes. Stir occasionally.

2. Add garlic and sugar and cook for 10 to 15 minutes.

3. Add stock, wine, and thyme; stir, and bring to a boil. Reduce heat to low and cook, uncovered, for 1 hour.

4. If you want a clear broth, pour through a strainer and add Cognac. If not, just add Cognac.

SALLY NIRENBERG

53

Parsnip with Sour Cream and Mustard

This soup is for parsnip lovers only, or for those willing to take a chance on the unknown. It is somewhat sweet and exotic and absolutely wonderful when chilled.

1 tablespoon unsalted butter
1 Spanish onion, coarsely chopped
1 pound parsnips, peeled and sliced
5 cups chicken stock
½–¾ teaspoon Dijon mustard
½ cup sour cream
Sour cream or plain yogurt for garnish

1. Melt butter over medium heat in a heavy-bottomed soup pot. Add onion and cook, covered, until golden, 10 to 15 minutes.

2. Add parsnips, chicken stock, and mustard and bring to a boil. Reduce heat to low and cook until parsnips are very soft, about 25 minutes.

3. Remove solids and place in a food processor or blender. Process until smooth, gradually adding remaining broth and sour cream.

4. Garnish each serving with a dollop of sour cream or yogurt.

Potato with Garlic

YIELD   7–8 CUPS

1¼ pounds potatoes, unpeeled, chopped (4–5 cups)
4–5 cups chicken stock
½–1 teaspoon garlic powder
¼ cup sour cream
½ cup heavy cream

1.   Cook potatoes with stock and garlic powder until mixture comes to a boil. Reduce heat to low and simmer until potatoes fall apart, about 20 minutes.

2.   Remove solids and place in a food processor or blender. Process until completely smooth, gradually adding broth, sour cream, and heavy cream.

I am generally opposed to using garlic powder, but for this soup I make an exception; fresh garlic is somehow too raw for this soothing and creamy blend.

Pumpkin with Bourbon

The flavor of this soup conjures up memories of pumpkin and sweet potato pie. Serve it at Thanksgiving or Christmas with the traditional fixings.

1 tablespoon unsalted butter
1 Spanish onion, coarsely chopped
1 pound fresh pumpkin, peeled, seeded, and diced
6 cups chicken or vegetable stock
1 teaspoon brown sugar
1 teaspoon dried thyme, or 1 tablespoon chopped fresh
1 teaspoon ground cinnamon
Juice of 1 orange
¼ cup bourbon

1.   Melt butter over low heat in a heavy-bottomed saucepan or stockpot. Add onion and cook, covered, until golden, 10 to 15 minutes.

2.   Add remaining ingredients and bring to a boil. Reduce heat and simmer for 25 to 30 minutes, or until pumpkin is tender.

3.   Remove solids and place in a food processor or blender. Process until completely smooth, gradually adding remaining broth.

VARIATION:

Substitute 1 pound sweet potatoes, peeled and chopped, for the pumpkin.

Tomato with Goat Cheese

YIELD 8 CUPS

This can be served either hot or cold. If you reduce the stock to three cups, it makes a great sauce for shrimp and/or pasta.

1 bunch leeks, including greens
1 tablespoon unsalted butter
2 16-ounce cans Italian plum tomatoes, coarsely chopped
5½ cups chicken or vegetable stock
1 tablespoon dried basil, or 3 tablespoons chopped fresh
½ pound goat cheese (such as Montrachet)
Freshly ground black pepper

1.   Cut off root end and 4 inches of greens of leeks and discard. Quarter them lengthwise and thinly slice. Soak them in several changes of water, being careful to get rid of all sand. Then chop well.

2.   Melt butter over medium heat in a heavy-bottomed saucepan or stockpot. Add leeks and cook, covered, until they have wilted, 15 to 20 minutes.

3.   Add tomatoes and their juice, stock, and basil and bring to a boil. Reduce heat to low and cook, uncovered, for 1½ hours.

4.   Remove pot from heat and gradually stir in goat cheese and pepper.

Triple Tomato

This soup is dedicated to Marc Levin, who always complained that my soups had too much "green stuff" in them. He wanted something that tasted great but had the familiarity of Campbell's.

1 tablespoon unsalted butter
1 large Spanish onion, coarsely chopped or thinly sliced
1 clove garlic, pressed or finely chopped
1 stalk celery, peeled and sliced
½ teaspoon curry powder
1 28-ounce can Italian plum tomatoes, chopped
4–5 cups chicken or vegetable stock
1 teaspoon dried basil, or 1 tablespoon chopped fresh
¼ teaspoon brown sugar
5 sun-dried tomatoes, packed in oil or dried
10 cherry tomatoes

1.   Melt butter over medium heat in a heavy-bottomed saucepan or stockpot. Add onion, garlic, celery, and curry powder and cook, covered, until vegetables are tender, about 20 minutes.

2.   Add plum tomatoes and their juice, stock, basil, and brown sugar and bring to a boil. Reduce heat to low and cook, partially covered, for 1½ hours.

3.   Remove solids and place in a food processor or blender with sun-dried tomatoes. Process until completely smooth, gradually adding remaining broth.

4.   Slice cherry tomatoes and float a few slices on top of each serving.

VARIATIONS:

Omit the sun-dried tomatoes, in which case you've made Double Tomato Soup.

Cream of Triple Tomato: Decrease the chicken stock by ½ cup and add ½ cup heavy cream or sour cream just prior to serving. For a lower calorie and fat version use ½ cup buttermilk or nonfat yogurt.

Omit basil and curry and replace with ¼ cup chopped fresh dill.

Creamy Vegetable

2 tablespoons unsalted butter
1 Spanish onion, finely chopped
10 cups assorted chopped vegetables (celery, carrots, yellow squash, parsnips, and zucchini are good)
8 cups vegetable or chicken stock
2 teaspoons dried tarragon, or 2 tablespoons chopped fresh
2 teaspoons fresh lemon juice
1 cup heavy cream

1.   Melt butter over low heat in a 4-quart pot. Add onion and cook, covered, until golden, 10 to 15 minutes.

2.   Add chopped vegetables, stock, and tarragon and bring to a boil. Reduce heat to low and cook until vegetables are tender, about 25 minutes.

3.   Remove solids and place in a food processor or blender. Process until smooth, gradually adding remaining broth, lemon juice, and heavy cream. Serve immediately.

This soup can be made with almost any combination of fresh vegetables. You can even use it as a vehicle for using up leftovers. I have chosen these particular ones because they are available all year round. This is equally good hot or chilled.

THE MOST REMARKABLE THING ABOUT MY MOTHER IS THAT FOR 30 YEARS SHE SERVED THE FAMILY NOTHING BUT LEFTOVERS. THE ORIGINAL MEAL HAS NEVER BEEN FOUND. Calvin Trillin

SALLY NIRENBERG
59

Watercress

This peppery green can sometimes be bitter, so be sure to find absolutely fresh, deep green watercress. This is an elegant soup that can be served as the first course to a special dinner.

1 tablespoon olive or canola oil
1 Spanish onion, coarsely chopped
2 shallots, finely chopped (about ¼ cup)
1 new red potato, unpeeled, cubed (about 2 cups)
8 cups vegetable or chicken stock
1 tomato, diced
1 teaspoon dried thyme, or 1 tablespoon chopped fresh
2 bunches watercress, finely chopped (about 4 cups packed)

1.   Heat oil over low flame in a 3-quart pot. Add onion and shallots and cook, covered, until vegetables are golden, 10 to 15 minutes.

2.   Add potato, stock, tomato, and thyme and bring to a boil. Reduce heat to medium and cook until potato is tender, about 35 minutes.

3.   Add watercress, cook for 5 minutes, and serve.

VARIATION:

Cream of Watercress: Substitute butter for the olive oil. After the soup has cooked, place the solids in a food processor and process until smooth, gradually adding ¾ cup heavy cream and ½ teaspoon ground cinnamon.

Curried Zucchini with Cream

1 tablespoon unsalted butter
1–2 medium Spanish onions, coarsely chopped
2–3 garlic cloves, pressed or finely chopped
1½ tablespoons curry powder
1–2 teaspoons peeled, finely chopped fresh ginger
3 large zucchini (2–2¼ pounds total), sliced
½ cup white rice
6 cups chicken stock
½ cup light or heavy cream

1.   Melt butter over medium heat in a heavy-bottomed saucepan or stockpot. Add onions, garlic, curry powder, ginger, and zucchini and cook, covered, until vegetables are tender, 20 to 25 minutes.

2.   Add rice and chicken stock and bring to a boil. Reduce heat to low and cook, partially covered, for 30 minutes.

3.   Remove solids and place in a food processor or blender. Process until completely smooth, gradually adding remaining broth and cream.

VARIATION:

Substitute for the zucchini an equal amount of cauliflower, broccoli, or carrots, alone or in combination.

There is a store in Westport, Connecticut, called Hay Day, part farmstand, part gourmet shop, part cheese store. I used to drive from New York to Boston a lot and always stopped in to get a cup of their Curried Zucchini Soup. Eventually, I made the drive less often, but as I could not stand to give up the soup, I had to make it myself; the result is my version of Hay Day's Curried Cream of Zucchini.

SALLY NIRENBERG

61

Zucchini Potato

I love potato soup, any kind will do; they are always so soothing and homey. This one has an especially nice flavor because of the rosemary and garlic. Feel free to substitute broccoli or cauliflower for the zucchini.

1 pound new red potatoes, unpeeled, sliced (about 2–3 cups)
2–2½ zucchini, sliced (about 1½ pounds)
4½ cups chicken stock
½ teaspoon dried rosemary, or 2 teaspoons chopped, fresh
2 garlic cloves, sliced
1½ cups heavy cream

1.   Combine all ingredients except cream in a 3-quart stockpot and bring to a boil. Reduce heat to medium and simmer until potatoes and zucchini are tender, about 20 minutes.

2.   Remove solids and place in a food processor or blender. Process until completely smooth, gradually adding remaining broth and cream.

NOTE: If you do not serve this soup right away, you may need to add additional stock: potato soups tend to thicken when they sit.

Bean Soups

In college my specialty was lentil soup and when I opened the Harvard Street store I had not gone any farther into soup making. The great thing about lentil soup was that, while it took what seemed like forever to cook, it more than made up for that by improving with age, being relatively inexpensive, and being so freeze-able. As I expanded my repertoire, I realized that this was essentially true for *all* bean soups.

A few things to keep in mind:

With the exception of the lentil and split-pea soups, all of the recipes in this book require presoaked beans. Unless you have a favored method, here is what I recommend:

1.   Soak the beans overnight. The reason for this is to prevent the bean skins from popping.
2.   In the morning or just prior to making your soup, cover the beans with water and bring to a boil. Let boil for 5 minutes and then reduce the heat to low and cook until the beans are tender.

3. Drain off the cooking liquid (it is the liquid and not the beans themselves that result in intestinal problems).

Salt toughens beans, radically increases cooking time, and decreases quality. Always soak and soften in unsalted water and cook with low-salt stocks.

Bean soups are all slow cooking and must never be rushed.

Feel free to substitute other kinds of beans, particularly in the chili recipes. New kinds of beans are constantly showing up on the shelves in supermarkets and particularly in health- and gourmet-food stores.

Although I generally prefer using dried beans because they taste fresher, I make an exception in the case of dark red kidney beans, which I prefer canned.

Spicy Black Bean

1 pound black turtle beans, soaked overnight
Water to cover
2 tablespoons olive oil
2 large Spanish onions, finely chopped
4 cloves garlic, pressed or finely chopped
1–2 teaspoons ground cumin
1–2 teaspoons chili powder
1½ teaspoons dried Greek oregano
½–1 teaspoon cayenne
8 cups water or low-salt chicken stock
½–1 teaspoon black pepper (optional)
¼ cup lime juice
1½ teaspoons brown sugar
Salt
Dry sherry
Chopped fresh cilantro
Sour cream

1.   An hour or two before you start the soup, put the black beans in a pot with the water. Bring to a boil. Reduce heat to medium and cook until soft, about 1 hour.

2.   Heat oil over low flame in a heavy-bottomed 4-quart soup

Making Black Bean Soup is a project; it is time-consuming and tends to need lots of adjustments, but it is well worth it. Every time—and there have been many—that I have tried to speed up the process, I have been sorry, particularly because I am always reminded by my friend Susan Schaub, who orders Black Bean Soup every time it's on the menu. If the soup is not prepared exactly right, just the way she had it the first time, she never hesitates to let me know.

Start this soup the day before you want to serve it; two days before is ideal.

The freshness of the dried spices is crucial; if yours have been in your cabinets for years, please, please throw them out and get replacements!

pot. Add onions, garlic, and spices and cook, covered, until onions are translucent, 10 to 15 minutes.

3.   Drain and rinse black beans and add to soup pot. Add water or stock and bring to a boil. Reduce heat to medium and cook, partially covered, for 2 hours, stirring frequently.

4.   After 2 hours, check to see if you need to add more water. If necessary, add 2 to 4 more cups and return to a boil. Reduce heat to low and cook, partially covered, for 2 hours.

5.   If you want a pureed soup, remove solids and place in a food processor or blender. Process until smooth, gradually adding liquid. Stir in pepper, lime juice, and brown sugar and return to pot. If you prefer your soup with more texture, simply skip this step. Cook over low heat until just heated through, about 5 minutes.

6.   Adjust seasonings and salt and add pepper to taste.

7.   Garnish each serving with sherry, chopped fresh cilantro, and a dollop of sour cream.

Black Bean and Ham

1½–2 cups black turtle beans
Water to cover
2 tablespoons olive or canola oil
1 large Spanish onion, coarsely chopped
1 large or 2 small carrots, peeled and sliced
1 stalk celery, including leaves, sliced
1 small zucchini, coarsely chopped
4 garlic cloves, pressed or finely chopped
2 teaspoons dried thyme
2–3 teaspoons chili powder
1 teaspoon dried Greek oregano
1 teaspoon crushed red pepper
12 cups low-salt chicken stock
2 cups coarsely chopped canned or fresh tomatoes
¼ pound smoked ham, sliced and chopped
1 tablespoon red wine vinegar
Salt

1.   Put black beans in a 4-quart pot with the water and bring to a boil. Reduce heat to medium and cook until needed in this recipe.

2.   Heat oil over low flame in a heavy-bottomed 6-quart soup pot. Add onion, carrots, celery, zucchini, garlic, and spices and cook, covered, until vegetables are tender, about 25 minutes.

3.   Add chicken stock and tomatoes and bring to a boil. Add beans. Reduce heat to medium and cook, uncovered, until beans are tender, about 1½ hours.

4.   Add ham and vinegar, stir, and let sit for 10 minutes. Salt to taste.

This recipe is the result of an attempt to copy a soup I had at The Harvest Restaurant in Cambridge. When I ordered the soup I expected something smooth, because I'd only had black beans cooked so long they fell apart. I was unexpectedly delighted by this chunky, spicy rendition.

Try it with white beans, too.

SALLY NIRENBERG

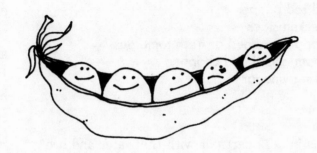

Black-Eyed Pea with Collard Greens

½ pound black-eyed peas
Water to cover
2 tablespoons olive or canola oil
1 large Spanish onion, coarsely chopped
1 carrot, peeled and sliced
1 stalk celery, sliced
2 cloves garlic, pressed or finely chopped
8 cups low-salt chicken or vegetable stock
1 cup dry white wine
1 teaspoon dried thyme
¼ teaspoon red pepper flakes
2 bay leaves
¾–1 pound collard greens, chopped

1.   Put black-eyed peas in a pot with the water and bring to a boil. Reduce heat to medium and cook until needed in this recipe.

2.   Heat oil over low flame in a heavy-bottomed 6-quart stock-pot. Add onion, carrot, celery, and garlic and cook, covered, until vegetables are tender, about 20 minutes.

3.   Add stock, wine, and spices and bring to a boil. Drain and rinse beans and add to soup pot. Reduce heat to medium and cook, partially covered, for 2 hours.

4.   Add chopped collard greens, stir, and cook for 45 minutes. Salt to taste and serve immediately.

VARIATION:

   You can use equivalent amounts of white beans and kale in place of the black-eyed peas and collard greens for a soup with a Portuguese (southern) flavor.

This recipe was inspired by Sally Belk, food editor at *Bon Appétit* magazine. Sally is Southern. I am Northern, not as patient, and do not have the Southern fondness for pork. My version, therefore, has both fewer steps and fewer ingredients. Perhaps this makes it altogether a different soup, but it's still a delicious one.

Curried Spinach and Lentil

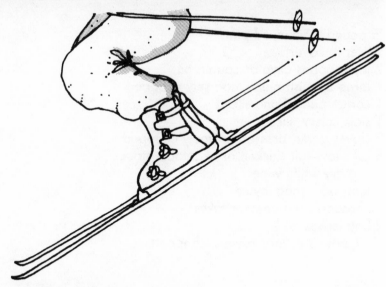

This is a hearty one-dish meal, especially wonderful to come in to after skiing or sledding. Put the soup on the stove in the morning and after a long and leisurely breakfast, go outside. When the cold becomes too much, your soup will be ready.

1 cup lentils, rinsed and picked over
1 Spanish onion, finely chopped
2 garlic cloves, pressed or finely chopped
2 carrots, peeled and diced
1 stalk celery, sliced
10–12 cups low-salt chicken or vegetable stock
1 tablespoon curry powder
1 large potato, diced (about 1½ cups)
1 10-ounce bag spinach, washed, stemmed, and coarsely chopped
1 tablespoon red wine vinegar
Salt
Sour cream or plain yogurt

1.   Place lentils, onion, garlic, carrots, celery, 6 cups stock, and curry powder in a soup pot and bring to a boil. Reduce heat to medium and cook, partially covered, for 2 hours.

2.   Add potato, spinach, and 4 cups more of stock and cook, uncovered, for 2 hours more.

3.   Add vinegar and, if necessary, more stock. Salt to taste.

4.   Serve with a dollop of sour cream or yogurt.

Lentil Barley

1 cup lentils, rinsed and picked over
4 scallions, including greens, sliced
1 carrot, peeled and sliced
2 stalks celery, including leaves, sliced
1 teaspoon dried Greek oregano
¼ cup barley, or white or brown rice
10–12 cups low-salt chicken, beef, or vegetable stock
1 16-ounce can whole peeled tomatoes, coarsely chopped
¼ cup dry red wine
Salt and pepper

1. Put all ingredients, except for last 3, in a 6-quart pot and bring to a boil.

2. Reduce heat to low and simmer, uncovered, for 2 hours. The soup should reduce by 20 to 25 percent.

3. Add tomatoes and wine, stir, and continue cooking for an additional 1 to 2 hours. Salt and pepper to taste.

There are thousands of recipes for lentil soup. This particular one emerged while I was stranded in a house in the Berkshires with a semistocked refrigerator and a house full of people begging for warmth and soup and nourishment.

Using brown rice instead of the more conventional barley adds a welcome, slightly nutty flavor.

Noah's Minestrone

2 teaspoons olive or canola oil
2 small onions, finely chopped
2 cloves garlic, pressed or finely chopped
2 stalks celery, peeled and sliced
2 carrots, peeled, quartered lengthwise, and sliced
2 zucchini, quartered lengthwise and sliced
2 yellow squash, quartered lengthwise and sliced
2 large tomatoes, diced
8 cups beef stock
2 cups chicken stock
2 teaspoons dried basil, or 2 tablespoons chopped fresh
2 handfuls (five-year-old size) dried white or kidney beans, about
    ½ cup
2 handfuls (five-year-old size) white rice, about ½ cup
Salt and pepper to taste

1. Heat oil over low flame in a 6-quart pot. Add onions, garlic, celery, carrots, zucchini, and yellow squash and cook, covered, until vegetables are tender, about 25 minutes.

2. Add remaining ingredients except rice, and bring to a boil. Reduce heat to low and cook, partially covered, for one hour.

3. Add rice and cook, partially covered, for an additional hour.

This soup was made to honor my friend Noah Levin, who, when I met him, was all of five years old, a formidable critic, and a blossoming gourmet.

Pasta e Fagioli

There are many versions of Pasta e Fagioli, Italian Pasta and Beans. Southern Italians make it differently than Northern Italians, and Italians in America make it yet another way. This is the American-in-America version, a synthesis of them all. Feel free to experiment with different kinds of beans and different shapes of pasta, but don't leave out the rosemary, it is especially wonderful here.

Serve this with a ham sandwich for the perfect meal.

1 tablespoon olive or safflower oil
1 onion, finely chopped
1 garlic clove, pressed or finely chopped
2 stalks celery, sliced
2 carrots, peeled and diced or sliced
1 cup kidney or white cannellini beans
½ cup tomato puree, or 1 tomato, chopped
10 cups low-salt chicken stock
½ cup dry white wine
1 bay leaf
1 teaspoon dried rosemary, or 1 tablespoon chopped fresh
¼ teaspoon dried thyme, or 1 teaspoon chopped fresh
¼ teaspoon dried basil, or 1 teaspoon chopped fresh
⅓ cup orzo (rice-shape pasta)
1 tablespoon chopped fresh parsley
Freshly grated Parmesan or Romano cheese

1. Heat oil over low flame in a 6-quart soup pot. Add onion, garlic, celery, and carrots and cook, covered, until vegetables are tender, about 20 minutes.

2. Add beans, tomato, chicken stock, wine, and herbs and bring to a boil. Reduce heat to low and cook, partially covered, for 2 hours.

3. Remove half the vegetables and place in a food processor or blender. Process briefly. Return to soup and bring to a boil

4. Add orzo and parsley, and cook until orzo is done, about 20 minutes.

5. Sprinkle with Parmesan or Romano cheese before serving.

VARIATION:

You can substitute any kind of small pasta for the orzo.

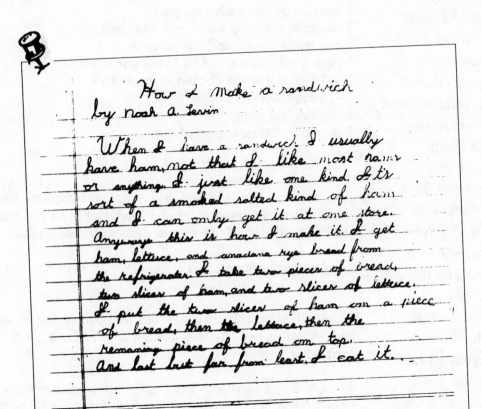

How to make a sandwich
by Noah A. Levin

When I have a sandwich I usually
have ham, not that I like most ham
or anything. I just like one kind. It's
sort of a smoked salted kind of ham
and I can only get it at one store.
Anyways this is how I make it. I get
ham, lettuce, and anadama rye bread from
the refrigerator. I take two pieces of bread,
two slices of ham, and two slices of lettuce.
I put the two slices of ham on a piece
of bread, then the lettuce, then the
remaining piece of bread on top.
And last but far from least, I eat it.

Portuguese Kale

Last summer I visited my friends Donna and Russ Robinson on Cape Cod and was reintroduced to Portuguese Kale Soup. Donna and I spent our days working very hard and very seriously on our tans. The fact that we were burning up at night did not prevent us from craving and eating some of this hot and spicy soup each and every evening.

Be sure to follow up with ice cream.

1 pound linguiça, or ½ pound linguiça and ½ pound chorizo
   sausages, sliced or diced
1 Spanish onion, finely chopped
7–8 garlic cloves, pressed or finely chopped
1 cup lentils, rinsed and picked over
1 pound kale, torn apart by hand, stems removed
12–14 cups low-salt chicken or beef stock
1–2 teaspoons red pepper flakes
1 cup dry red wine
1 pound potatoes, unpeeled, cubed
Salt

1. Cook sausages and chopped onion over medium heat until sausages are rendered of fat and onion begins to wilt and starts to brown slightly, about 20 minutes. Stir occasionally.

2. Add garlic cloves, and cook, covered, over low heat for 10 minutes.

3. Add lentils, kale, 10 cups stock, red pepper flakes, and wine and bring to a boil. Reduce heat to low and cook, partially covered, for 1 hour.

4. Add 2 to 4 cups additional stock and potatoes; stir and continue to cook, uncovered, over low heat for at least 2 hours. Salt to taste.

NOTES: Portuguese Kale Soup ages well; it can be made the day ahead and gently reheated.

If you are going to freeze all or some of this soup, omit the potatoes. Add them after the soup is fully defrosted: cook over low heat for 1 hour.

VARIATION:

Add one 16-ounce can Italian plum tomatoes when you add the kale.

M - 1957

Split Pea with Lemon

For years the only split-pea soup I made had the double whammy of smoked meat and heavy cream. While that version is somehow both rich and delicate, the cholesterol- and calorie-conscious complained, and what follows is the result.

2 teaspoons canola or olive oil
1 Spanish onion, finely chopped
½ pound carrots, peeled, quartered lengthwise, and sliced
1 teaspoon dried tarragon, or 1 tablespoon chopped fresh
1 pound split peas, rinsed and picked over
8–10 cups low-salt chicken or vegetable stock
2 tablespoons lemon juice
Salt

1. Heat oil over low flame in a heavy-bottomed soup pot. Add onion and cook, covered, until golden, about 15 minutes.

2. Add carrots, tarragon, split peas, and 8 cups stock; bring to a boil. Reduce heat to low and cook, partially covered, until peas have fallen apart, about 2 hours.

3. After 1 hour, check to see if you need to add more stock. If so, add 2 cups.

4. Remove from heat and stir in lemon juice. Salt to taste.

NOTE: If you serve this soup on the following day, you will need to add more stock, as the soup is guaranteed to thicken over-night.

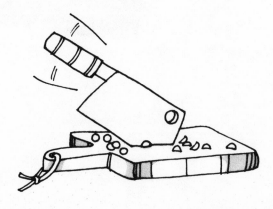

Split Pea with Smoked Turkey and Cream

YIELD 12–14 CUPS

1 tablespoon unsalted butter
1 Spanish onion, finely chopped
2–3 small potatoes, unpeeled, diced
1 pound (2¼ cups) split peas, rinsed and picked over
2 teaspoons dried thyme, or 1 tablespoon chopped fresh
14 cups low-salt chicken stock
¼ pound smoked turkey, chopped or finely sliced
¾ cup heavy cream
1 teaspoon ground nutmeg

This is the lightest, most delicate pea soup I've ever tasted.

1. Melt butter over low heat in a heavy-bottomed soup pot. Add onion and cook, covered, until golden, 10 to 15 minutes.

2. Add potatoes, split peas, 1 teaspoon dried thyme, and chicken stock; bring to a boil. Add smoked turkey, reduce heat to low, and cook, covered, for 1½ hours. Stir occasionally.

3. Remove cover and simmer until peas have completely fallen apart and soup is of desired thickness, about 45 minutes. Stir occasionally.

4. Blend in cream, remaining 1 teaspoon thyme, and nutmeg and serve.

NOTE: This soup can be frozen prior to adding cream. Defrost, reheat, and finish recipe.

White Bean with Basil

White beans are my favorite beans to cook with. After they cook for a while, the broth becomes sweet and the beans take on a texture unlike anything else.

This is a soup for a blustery, cold day; you'll be thankful you made such a big pot.

1 tablespoon olive or safflower oil
1 Spanish onion, finely chopped
1 garlic clove, pressed or finely chopped
8 cups low-salt chicken stock
1 tablespoon dried basil, or 1 tablespoon chopped fresh, plus whole leaves for garnish
½ teaspoon dried Greek oregano, or 1 ½ teaspoons chopped fresh
1 16-ounce can peeled whole tomatoes, chopped
1 pound white beans, soaked overnight, quick cooked, and drained
1 tablespoon red wine vinegar
Chopped fresh tomatoes

1.   Heat oil over low flame in a heavy-bottomed soup pot. Add onion and garlic and cook, covered, until onion is golden, about 10 minutes.

2.   Add stock, herbs, canned tomatoes, and beans; bring to a boil. Reduce heat to low and cook, partially covered, until beans have fallen apart, 2 to 3 hours.

3.   Add vinegar just prior to serving.

4.   Garnish with fresh whole basil leaves and chopped fresh tomatoes.

White Bean and Vegetable with Garlic and Rosemary

1 pound (2¼ cups dried) white cannellini beans, soaked overnight, quick cooked, and drained
2 teaspoons dried rosemary, or 2 tablespoons chopped fresh, plus extra for garnish
2 garlic cloves
1 Spanish onion, coarsely chopped
2 stalks celery, halved lengthwise and sliced
2 carrots, quartered lengthwise and sliced
1 large potato, cubed (1½ cups)
16 cups low-salt chicken stock
1 16-ounce can whole peeled tomatoes, drained and chopped
Chopped fresh parsley, about 2–4 tablespoons
Salt

1.   Put all ingredients, except tomatoes, parsley, and salt, in a 6-quart pot and bring to a boil. Reduce heat to low and cook, partially covered, for 1–2 hours, or until beans are very, very soft.

2.   Add tomatoes and continue to cook for 1 ½ hours, or until soup thickens.

3.   Season with chopped parsley and salt to taste.

4.   Garnish with fresh rosemary.

VARIATION:

You can halve the amount of white beans and make this a brothier soup.

The inspiration for this soup was a vegetable dip described to me by my friends Jan and Bruce Spitz. The ingredients in the soup are essentially the same as in the dip, but I like to think that this is an even better application.

Chicken Soups

There is really nothing like chicken soup.

I recently made a tour of all the chicken rotisseries and delicatessens in my neighborhood (you'd be amazed at how many that adds up to; after all, this isn't New York City), and what I found was that even bad chicken soup isn't that bad.

Some were clearly made from scratch and some were made from commercial bases; some were loaded with chunks of chicken and some with vegetables; others were brothy. What I discovered was that people, easygoing, nice people, are generally very, very opinionated about chicken soup.

I have tried to include a variety of chicken soups, taking into account how hard it is to replicate *your* mother's version.

Avgolemono

8 cups strong chicken stock
⅓ cup orzo or rice
8 large egg yolks
¼–⅓ cup *fresh* lemon juice
Fresh parsley or dill

1. Bring chicken stock to a boil in a 3-quart soup pot. Add orzo, reduce heat, and simmer for 15 minutes.

2. Whip egg yolks and lemon juice together in a bowl (the mixture tends to come out a little better if done by hand, rather than in a food processor or blender).

3. Very gradually, add some of stock mixture to lemon mixture, being very careful not to let eggs curdle. Return mixture to soup pot and cook over very low heat for 10 minutes. Keep whisking until all stock is combined with eggs.

4. Chop parsley or dill and sprinkle in the soup. Let sit for 15 minutes.

This soup is Greek in origin but comes to me from my Aunt Mary, who is not Greek at all. When I first opened the Harvard Street store, she came up to visit; when we ran out of soup on a very cold afternoon, she whipped this one up and saved the day. Avgolemono is a great soup: it is not only delicious, it is inexpensive, easy, and quick. It has helped me survive many a flu season.

Chicken with Ginger and Dill

This recipe was hesitantly given to me by my friend and running partner, Carol Lesser; she did not believe that her recipe for chicken soup could be better than mine. Clearly, they are equals.

1 tablespoon unsalted butter
1 small onion, finely chopped
1 stalk celery, sliced
1 carrot, peeled and sliced or diced
1 parsnip, peeled and sliced or diced
1 teaspoon peeled, finely chopped fresh ginger
1 clove garlic, pressed or finely chopped
10 cups chicken stock
1 large potato, peeled and diced, or ¼ cup rice, barley, or small
      pasta (such as alphabet or orzo)
½–1 pound boneless, skinless chicken breasts, diced
1–2 tablespoons chopped fresh dill
Salt and pepper

1.   Melt butter over low heat in a 4-quart soup pot. Add onion, vegetables, ginger, and garlic and cook, covered, until vegetables are tender, about 15 minutes.

2.   Add chicken stock and potato (or rice, etc.) and bring to a boil. Reduce heat to low and simmer, uncovered, for 1 hour.

3.   Add chicken and dill and continue to simmer until chicken is completely cooked, 15 to 20 minutes. Add salt and pepper to taste.

Chicken with Rosemary

1–2 tablespoons unsalted butter or olive oil
1 Spanish onion, finely chopped
2 stalks celery, sliced or diced
2 carrots, peeled and sliced or diced
10 cups chicken stock
1 teaspoon dried marjoram, or 1 tablespoon chopped fresh
1 teaspoon dried rosemary, or 1 tablespoon chopped fresh
¼ teaspoon dried thyme, or 1 teaspoon chopped fresh
½ cup rice or small pasta (such as alphabets or orzo)
1 pound boneless, skinless chicken breasts, diced

1. Melt butter or oil over low heat in a 6-quart soup pot. Add onion, celery, and carrots and cook, covered, until vegetables are tender, about 15 minutes.

2. Add chicken stock and herbs and bring to a boil.

3. Add rice or pasta, reduce heat to low, and cook, uncovered, for 1 hour.

4. Add chicken, stir, and simmer until it is thoroughly cooked, about 20 minutes.

After spending hours and hours every day making soup, I can still come home and make this one. It is almost effortless to prepare, and I never tire of its taste.

SALLY NIRENBERG

Chicken with Tarragon Cream

This beautiful soup has little flecks of color throughout. It is elegant enough for an autumn wedding.

2 tablespoons unsalted butter
1 Spanish onion, coarsely chopped
1 carrot, peeled and sliced
1 stalk celery, including leaves, sliced
1 tomato, quartered and seeded
8 cups chicken stock
1 tablespoon dried tarragon, or 3 tablespoons chopped fresh
1 pound boneless, skinless chicken breasts, cut into strips
1 cup heavy cream

1. Melt butter over low heat in a heavy-bottomed soup pot. Add onion, carrot, and celery and cook, covered, until vegetables are tender, about 15 minutes, stirring occasionally.

2. Add tomato and chicken stock. Bring to a boil.

3. Remove vegetables and place in a food processor or blender. Process until broth looks like confetti and return to soup pot.

4. Add tarragon, chicken, and cream; blend and simmer over low heat until chicken is cooked, about 20 minutes. Serve immediately.

Matzoh Ball Soup

This recipe wasn't handed down to me from *my* grandmother, it was handed down to my friend Donna Levin from her mother and to her mother from *her* mother, Helen Geller. I am honored to include it here and wish only that I could claim it as my own, or at least as my own grandmother's.

1 4-pound chicken, fat removed
12 cups water
1 teaspoon kosher salt
2 Spanish onions, halved
1 stalk celery, halved lengthwise
1 carrot, peeled and halved
1 parsnip, peeled and halved
Matzoh Balls (see recipe below)
Few sprigs parsley
Few sprigs dill
Salt and pepper

1. Pour 3 changes of boiling water over chicken to clean it thoroughly.

2. Cut up chicken and put it in a soup pot with water, salt, and vegetables. Bring to a boil, reduce heat to medium, and cook for 1½ hours. Start the matzoh balls at this point.

3. Add parsley and dill and cook for 30 minutes more.

4. Strain the soup (reserving cooked chicken for another use, if desired), skim off fat, and add salt and pepper to taste.

NOTE: This broth makes a perfect chicken stock for use in other soups.

Matzoh Balls

6 eggs, separated
2 teaspoons kosher salt
1 cup plus 2 tablespoons matzoh meal

1.   Beat egg whites until stiff. Set aside.

2.   Add salt to egg yolks and beat. Add matzoh meal and combine with whites.

3.   Chill for 45 minutes and form into 8 to 12 matzoh balls.

4.   Boil a pot of water and add chilled matzoh balls. Cook for 45 minutes and add to hot chicken soup.

SALLY NIRENBERG

Mexican Avgolemono

I call this Mexican Avgolemono because it's made like a classic Avgolemono but with Mexican flavors. Serve this as a first course, followed by a peppery, marinated steak and a citrus and tomato salad.

8 cups rich chicken stock
½ cup orzo or white rice
½ cup packed fresh cilantro leaves, washed well and chopped
8 egg yolks
½–1 teaspoon garlic powder
½ cup lime juice
Pinch cayenne

1. Bring chicken stock to a rolling boil in a 4-quart soup pot. Add orzo or rice and let cook over medium heat for 15 minutes.

2. While broth is cooking, blend remaining ingredients.

3. Gradually add some of the hot broth to egg mixture and then gradually add mixture to remaining broth. Let sit for 5 minutes and serve.

Mexican Chicken Soup with Cocoa

2 tablespoons olive oil
8 cloves garlic, pressed or finely chopped
2 tablespoons all-purpose white flour
12 cups chicken stock
3 cups diced fresh or canned tomatoes, drained
1 bunch scallions, including greens, thinly sliced
¼ teaspoon crushed red pepper
1 teaspoon unsweetened cocoa powder
¼ teaspoon dried Greek oregano
⅛ teaspoon ground cumin
2 whole chicken breasts (1½ pounds), chopped or sliced
6 sprigs parsley or cilantro, coarsely chopped

1.   Heat oil over low heat in a large heavy-bottomed soup pot. Add garlic and cook, covered, until golden, about 10 minutes.

2.   Slowly add flour, stirring constantly, until thick and paste-like. Cook the roux for 3 to 5 minutes, stirring constantly. Add stock very gradually, whisking with each addition.

3.   Add vegetables and spices and bring to a boil. Reduce heat to low and cook for 1½ hours.

4.   Add chicken and parsley or cilantro, stir, and simmer until chicken is cooked, about 20 minutes.

Mulligatawny

After I graduated from college, I lived in San Francisco and worked near a restaurant that served Mulligatawny Soup. I ordered it whenever it was on the menu and eventually figured out how to make it myself. Because it seemed exotic, I'd assumed it was complicated. I was wrong; it isn't.

2 tablespoons unsalted butter
1 Spanish onion, chopped
1 Granny Smith apple, unpeeled, cored, and chopped
1 carrot, peeled, halved lengthwise, and thinly sliced
1–2 tablespoons curry powder
1 fresh or canned tomato, diced
10 cups chicken stock
¼ cup unsweetened shredded coconut
1 pound boneless, skinless chicken breasts, diced or shredded

1.   Melt butter over low heat in a heavy-bottomed soup pot. Add onion, apple, carrot, and curry and cook, covered, until vegetables are tender, about 10 minutes.

2.   Add tomato and chicken stock and bring to a boil. Reduce heat to low and simmer for 1 hour.

3.   Remove half the solids and place in a food processor. Process briefly and return to soup pot.

4.   Add coconut and chicken, stir, and simmer until chicken is thoroughly cooked, about 15 minutes.

VARIATION:

Decrease amount of stock used by ½ cup and add ½ cup light or heavy cream just prior to serving.

Vegetable with Smoked Turkey, Romaine, and Parmesan

YIELD ABOUT 10 CUPS

¼ pound slab bacon
1 carrot, peeled and chopped
1 Spanish onion, finely chopped; or 4 scallions, chopped
1 stalk celery, chopped
1 parsnip or turnip, peeled and chopped
1 clove garlic, pressed or finely chopped
8 Italian plum tomatoes, drained and crushed
1 quart chicken stock
1 quart water
¼ pound smoked turkey breast
½ cup tiny pasta pieces (such as orzo or broken spaghetti)
6 leaves romaine lettuce, chopped
½ cup grated Parmesan cheese
Pepper to taste

1. Cook bacon; drain and chop. Reserve 2 tablespoons of fat and add next 4 ingredients. Cook over low heat with lid on for 8 minutes.

2. Add garlic and tomatoes and bring to a boil.

3. Add stock, water, turkey, and pasta and simmer gently for 10 minutes.

4. Add romaine and cook until it is completely wilted, approximately 10 minutes. Serve immediately, sprinkled with Parmesan and pepper.

VARIATIONS:

Leave out the tomatoes: the first time that I made this I forgot them.
Substitute chicken or ham for the smoked turkey.
Substitute spinach for the romaine.

This unusually delicious soup came to me from the mother of my friend and Harpoon Ale salesman, Mark. In the first year that I knew Mark, every time he came into my shop he described a strange and intriguing soup made by his mother. After months of promises, he brought in the recipe; here follows Patty Sampson's recipe, word for word. Almost.

I don't salt this soup; it is full of salty ingredients. Don't add salt until you've tasted the finished product.

Fish Soups

In the past seven years, I have probably made soup with fish no more than twenty times. This is the result of two things: one, both of my stores have been next door to fish restaurants, and two, but perhaps more important, I do not think that soup is a great vehicle for fish or seafood. I prefer fish in its more whole state.

I do, however, make an exception for both clams and mussels, because they are so small to start with, and while less delicate than other fish, they absorb flavors well. I don't include instructions for cleaning and shelling either, because I buy them already cleaned and shelled and suggest you do the same.

there are always
more fish in the sea,
not as cute nor as
rich but fish
nevertheless.

Chinese fortune cookie
wisdom.

Mussel Chowder

YIELD   10 CUPS

2 tablespoons unsalted butter
1 Spanish onion, finely chopped
2 tablespoons all-purpose white flour
¼ cup dry white wine
1 pound potatoes, unpeeled and cubed
4 cups chicken or fish stock
1 tomato, diced
¼ teaspoon dried thyme, or ¾ teaspoon fresh
2 tablespoons chopped fresh parsley
½ cup heavy cream
1 pound mussels, shelled

1.   Melt butter over low heat in a 4-quart soup pot. Add onion and cook, covered, for 10 minutes. Slowly sprinkle in flour, stirring all the time.

2.   Gradually add wine and cook for 5 minutes. Add potatoes, stock, tomato, and thyme. Bring to a boil. Reduce heat to low and cook until potatoes are tender, about 20 minutes.

3.   Stir in parsley, heavy cream, and mussels; continue to simmer until mussels are cooked through, about 10 minutes. Serve immediately.

New England Clam Chowder

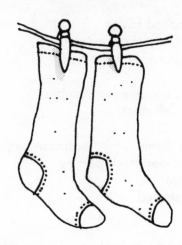

Bostonians are very particular about their clam chowder. It took me years before I included it on my menu. I desperately tried to leave out the flour but found that it was necessary for the soup's consistency. After much experimentation, I discovered that the tried and true was the best. This won't knock your socks off, but you will feel like you've arrived home: it is creamy, full of flavor and comfort.

¼ cup unsalted butter
1 Spanish onion, finely chopped
2 cloves garlic, pressed or finely chopped
¼ cup all-purpose white flour
8 cups clam juice, or 4 cups clam juice and 4 cups water
2–3 potatoes, unpeeled, diced (about 2 cups)
2 stalks celery, thinly sliced
1 teaspoon dried thyme, or 1 tablespoon fresh
1 cup light or heavy cream
1 pound raw clams, shelled

1.   Melt butter over low heat in a heavy-bottomed soup pot. Add onion and garlic and cook, covered, until golden, about 15 minutes. Gradually add flour, stirring all the time.

2.   Gradually add clam juice, and when it is thoroughly incorporated, add potatoes, celery, and thyme, and bring to a boil. Reduce heat to low and cook until potatoes are tender, about 20 minutes.

3.   Gradually stir in cream and clams and continue to simmer until clams are thoroughly cooked, about 10 minutes. Be very careful not to overcook them. Serve immediately.

Spicy Clam and Vegetable

2 tablespoons olive oil
1 Spanish onion, finely chopped
4 cloves garlic, pressed or finely chopped
1 small zucchini, coarsely chopped
1 large potato, unpeeled, diced (about 1 cup)
½ teaspoon dried oregano, or 1½ teaspoons fresh
½ teaspoon crushed red pepper flakes
1 cup dry white wine
4 cups water
4 cups clam juice
16 ounces shelled clams, in juice
1 tablespoon chopped fresh parsley

This is a great spicy soup. Serve it with lots of Italian bread for soaking up the last drops.

1.   Heat oil over low flame in a heavy-bottomed soup pot. Add onion and garlic and cook, covered, until golden, 10–15 minutes.

2.   Add zucchini, potato, oregano, pepper flakes, wine, water, and clam juice and bring to a boil. Reduce heat to low and cook for 45 minutes.

3.   Stir in clams and parsley and simmer until clams are thoroughly cooked, about 5 minutes. Serve immediately.

SALLY NIRENBERG

Chili

The first time that I ever made or, I'm embarrassed to say, ever tasted chili was when I made Spicy Sausage Chili a few years ago. I immediately liked what I had made, but as I really didn't know what I was doing and had no frame of reference, I had to sit back and wait anxiously for a response.

Of course, there were the expected mixed reviews. Almost all were positive, but some people found it too spicy, others didn't like the use of sausages, others wanted vegetarian chili. So I went back into the kitchen and experimented some more.

The following chilies all have similar bases, although they do differ in some very distinct ways. If there are particular beans that you especially like, add them. If you hate others, leave them out.

Black Bean Chili

This is the prettiest chili. I've always wanted to have a party where I served only black and white food; I've never quite gotten around to it, but I know that this would be perfect, served with a dollop of goat cheese.

4 cups black turtle beans, soaked overnight
Water to cover
¼ cup olive oil
2 Spanish onions, coarsely chopped
4 cloves garlic, pressed or finely chopped
2 tablespoons ground cumin
2 tablespoons dried Greek oregano
2 tablespoons chili powder
2 bay leaves
4 1-pound cans whole tomatoes, in their juice, coarsely chopped
6–8 cups water or chicken stock
2 teaspoons salt
Chopped fresh cilantro
Sour cream

1.   Put black beans in a pot with water and bring to a boil. Reduce heat and let cook for about 1 hour (the beans should be almost soft).

2.   Heat oil over low flame in a heavy-bottomed soup pot. Add onions, garlic, and spices and cook, covered, until translucent, about 10 minutes.

3.   Add remaining ingredients, except beans, stir, and bring to a boil. Drain and rinse black beans and add to pot. Return to a boil. Reduce heat to low and let cook, partially covered, for 2 hours.

4.   Serve with fresh cilantro and big heaps of sour cream.

Chili with Eggplant and Beef

2 tablespoons olive oil
2 Spanish onions, coarsely chopped
3 cloves garlic, pressed or finely chopped
1 1–1½-pound eggplant, cubed (4–4½ cups)
2 teaspoons ground cumin
2–4 teaspoons chili powder
2 teaspoons dried Greek oregano
1 teaspoon ground cinnamon
1–2 teaspoons red pepper flakes
1–1½ pounds lean ground beef
3–4 1-pound cans dark red kidney beans, drained and rinsed
   (see Notes)
1 28-ounce can whole tomatoes, coarsely cut
1 28-ounce can crushed tomatoes
1 cup dry red wine
Garnishes: sliced scallions, yellow and red peppers, black or Greek
   olives, chopped fresh tomatoes, sour cream, grated Cheddar
   cheese (optional)

The Mediterranean meets Mexico.

1.   Heat oil over low flame in a heavy-bottomed soup pot. Add onions and garlic and cook, covered, until golden, about 10 minutes. Add eggplant and spices and sauté for 5 minutes.

2.   Add beef, stirring until brown.

3.   Add kidney beans, tomatoes, and wine; stir and cook, covered, for 30 minutes. Remove the lid and cook for another 1 to 2 hours, depending on how thick you want the chili to be. Stir frequently. Adjust spices to taste.

4.   Garnish with any combination of sliced scallions, fresh yellow and red peppers, black or Greek olives, chopped fresh tomatoes, sour cream, and Cheddar cheese.

NOTES: You must use *dark* red kidney beans: they are the only ones that can stand up to this amount of cooking and still retain their shape.

   It is also very important to use fresh dried spices. If yours have been sitting in your cabinets for years, throw them out!

SALLY NIRENBERG

Harpoon Chili

The best way to make this chili is with lots of friends; give each a Harpoon to drink and a job to do.

2 tablespoons olive oil
1 purple onion or 1 large leek, coarsely chopped
1 Spanish onion, coarsely chopped
4 cloves garlic, pressed or finely chopped
2–3 teaspoons chili powder
2–3 teaspoons crushed chili flakes
1–2 tablespoons ground cumin
1 small (¾–1 pound) eggplant, peeled and diced, or 2 zucchini, diced (3–4 cups)
1 cup dried white or garbanzo beans, soaked overnight and quick cooked; or 2½–3 cups canned
1 cup dried black beans, soaked overnight and quick cooked; or 2½–3 cups canned
2 1-pound cans dark red kidney beans, drained and rinsed
1–2 12-ounce bottles Harpoon ale
1 tablespoon dried Greek oregano
2 20-ounce cans whole tomatoes, coarsely chopped
1–1½ pounds skinless, boneless chicken breasts, poached and sliced
1 red pepper, cored, seeded, and cut into strips
1 green pepper, cored, seeded, and cut into strips
Goat cheese
Chopped fresh cilantro

1.   Heat oil over low flame in a heavy-bottomed stockpot. Add onion or leek, garlic, and spices and cook, covered, until golden, about 15 minutes.

2.   Add eggplant and cook, covered, for 15 minutes, stirring occasionally.

3.   Add beans, Harpoon ale, oregano, and tomatoes. Cook, covered, over medium heat for 30 minutes. Reduce heat to low and cook for 2 to 3 hours, partly covered, making sure all beans are completely soft.

4.   Add chicken and peppers and cook until just heated.

5.   Serve with a dollop of goat cheese and fresh cilantro.

NOTE: If you want to make vegetarian chili, omit the chicken.

Spicy Sausage Chili

I gave this recipe to five different friends to test. One said that it was not spicy enough and that she had to add a lot more cayenne and then some Tabasco. Another complained that her mouth was burning up. The other three thought that it was just perfect and that the other two were nuts. The quantities of spices are meant as guidelines; be sure to adjust them to your own taste.

1 pound spicy Italian sausage
¼ cup water
1 purple onion, coarsely chopped
1 Spanish onion, coarsely chopped
2–4 cloves garlic, pressed or finely chopped
2–4 teaspoons chili powder
2–4 teaspoons red pepper flakes
1–2 tablespoons ground cumin
2 tablespoons unsweetened cocoa powder
3 16-ounce cans whole tomatoes
2 16-ounce cans dark red kidney beans, drained and rinsed
½ cup dried white beans, soaked overnight and quick cooked
½ cup dried black beans, soaked overnight and quick cooked
1 red pepper, cored, seeded, and chopped
1 yellow or green pepper, cored, seeded, and chopped
Garnishes: sour cream, chopped fresh cilantro, grated Cheddar cheese, chopped scallions

1.   Put sausage and water in a soup pot and cook over high heat until sausage begins to fry in its own fat. Reduce heat to medium and cook until sausage browns, about 10 minutes. Remove sausage and set aside.

2.   Add onions to pot and cook over medium heat, until onions have softened, about 10 minutes. Slice cooked sausage into thin coins and add to pot. Add garlic, spices, and cocoa; stir and cook over low heat for 5 minutes.

3.   Add tomatoes and beans and cook, covered, for 2 hours.

4.   Stir in peppers and continue to cook, uncovered, over low heat for 35 to 45 minutes. Add additional spices if desired.

5.   Serve with bowls of sour cream, chopped fresh cilantro, Cheddar cheese, and chopped scallions.

Stews

Most of the following stews (except for Cassoulet) originated as fillings for potpies. I had tired of making chicken potpie and wanted to try something more unusual. While excellent as fillings, I found that each and every one of these recipes could stand alone.

If you want to use any of the stews as a potpie filling, here's my favorite topping dough:

1½ cups unbleached white flour
¼ teaspoon salt
¼ teaspoon sugar
¼ teaspoon ground nutmeg
½ cup margarine, butter, or solid shortening, or any combination
3 tablespoons ice water

1. Combine dry ingredients in a medium-size bowl.

2. Cut in shortening with 2 knives or a pastry blender until mixture resembles coarse cornmeal. Add ice water and mix until dough forms a ball.

3. Roll dough to fit top of dish(es), about ¼ inch thick. Bake at 350° until top is golden brown and filling is heated through.

SALLY NIRENBERG

YIELD   ENOUGH FOR ONE 9-INCH POTPIE OR 3–4 3-INCH RAMEKINS

Beef Carbonnade

My friend Sharon Briggs used to cook with me in the early days at Harvard Street. Now she lives in Nantucket with her family and travels about, but she hasn't forgotten me. Every trip produces a recipe.

This is essentially a classic Belgian carbonnade with some very nice additions.

¼ pound bacon, chopped
2½ pounds beef chuck, cut into small cubes and patted dry with a paper towel
2 large Spanish onions, coarsely chopped
1 tablespoon brown sugar
½ pound turnips, peeled and diced
½ pound carrots, peeled and sliced
½ pound potatoes, peeled and diced
1 tablespoon dried thyme, or 3 tablespoons chopped fresh thyme (see Note)
½ cup all-purpose white flour
2 12-ounce bottles beer (preferably dark and/or very flavorful)
1 cup rich beef stock

1.   Cook bacon in a skillet until rendered of all fat. Remove and set aside. Heat bacon fat until very hot, add beef a few pieces at a time and brown on all sides; set aside.

2.   Add onions and sugar to the bacon fat and cook until onions have caramelized.

3.   Add vegetables and thyme and cook, covered, over low heat for 20 minutes.

4.   Gradually add flour, stirring constantly.

5.   Gradually add beer and beef stock. Add reserved bacon and beef, stir, and cook over low heat until beef is tender, about 2 hours.

CRITICAL NOTE: My friend Peter Sistrom asked me for a great recipe for an important dinner party. He wanted something absolutely tried and true; a guarantee, no complications. I gave him this recipe, and my incomplete instructions almost ruined his party (not our friendship, I prayed). What I learned was that there was such a thing as powdered thyme and that it should not be used. Use dried or fresh. I also learned to warn the cook not to taste this in its initial stages, or at least to be prepared to taste the bitterness of the beer. Not to worry; the bitterness cooks out and the flavor remains.

Cassoulet

I had always wanted to try cassoulet. I thought that it sounded like a great dish, but I hesitated because it was traditionally made with meats that I couldn't quite stomach. My search ended at Lucky's, a restaurant in Providence, Rhode Island. On the menu: Winter Cassoulet with chicken, sausage, and pork chops. All acceptable to me. I was absolutely amazed. After days and days of exploration, I came up with this recipe, which approximates Lucky's.

Accompany

½ cup olive oil
½ cup all-purpose white flour
2 Spanish onions, finely chopped
2 carrots, peeled and diced
2 stalks celery, diced
6–8 garlic cloves, pressed or finely chopped
2 spicy Italian sausages
¼ cup water
1 pork chop
2 whole chicken breasts
1½ cups dry red wine
3–3½ cups chicken stock
1½ pounds white cannellini beans, soaked overnight
1½ teaspoons ground nutmeg
1½ tablespoons dried thyme, or 4½ tablespoons fresh
2 bay leaves
Chopped fresh parsley mixed with bread crumbs

1. Heat oil over high flame in a 6-quart stockpot until it sizzles. Slowly whisk in flour. Be very careful when you do this (you may want to stand back at first). Cook over high heat until mixture becomes dark red, almost black. This will take about 20 minutes; stir with a whisk constantly, in order to prevent flour from burning.

2. Reduce heat to low and add onions, carrots, and celery. The oil will sizzle when you do this, so do it gently. After 10 minutes, add garlic. Sauté for an additional 10 minutes.

3. Prick sausages with a fork and put them in a frying pan with water. Cook over high heat until they fry in their own fat. Remove sausages and set aside.

4.   Leave fat in the pan and cook pork chop. Remove pork chop and cook chicken. Cut meats into serving pieces (you can make them bite size or leave them whole) and set aside.

5.   Add wine, stock, beans, and spices to vegetables, stir, and cook over low heat for 2 hours.

6.   Add meats and place entire mixture in an ovenproof casserole. Sprinkle mixture of parsley and bread crumbs over top and put in a 350° oven. After 30 minutes, bread crumbs should have formed a crust. Push this down into the beans. Repeat this step twice; the third time do not push bread crumbs back in, leave the crust.

Cassoulet with a salad that has lots of tomatoes in it, and ice cold beer.

Classic Beef Stew

This is a hearty and rich stew. When I make it in the store, I never seem to make enough—it pulls the chills right out of your body. Always keep some on hand in the winter; it freezes well.

2 tablespoons olive oil or additional bacon or fat
2 large Spanish onions, coarsely chopped
4 garlic cloves, pressed or finely chopped
1 pound celery (about ½ bunch), sliced
1 pound carrots, peeled and sliced
¼ pound bacon, chopped
2½ pounds beef chuck, cut into cubes
½–1 cup all-purpose white flour
2 cups dry red wine
2 cups beef stock
1 16-ounce can Italian plum tomatoes, coarsely chopped
1 tablespoon dried thyme, or 3 tablespoons chopped fresh thyme
1½ pound potatoes, unpeeled, cut into cubes

1.   Heat oil or fat over low flame in a large stockpot. Add onions, garlic, celery, and carrots and cook, covered, until vegetables are tender, about 25 minutes.

2.   While vegetables are sautéeing, cook bacon in a large skillet until rendered of all fat; remove bacon and set aside.

3.   Coat beef cubes with flour and brown in bacon fat at a very high heat. You will need to do this in 2 to 3 batches.

4.   As the meat browns, add it to the sautéed vegetables. When all beef is browned, slowly add wine to pan, scraping bottom. Add mixture to stewpot.

5.   Slowly add beef stock. Stir in tomatoes and their juice and thyme. Cook over low heat until beef is tender, about 2 hours.

6.   Boil potatoes in a separate pot and add to stew about 30 minutes prior to serving, or if you wish, serve on the side.

Curried Beef Stew

¼ cup all-purpose white flour
¼ cup curry powder
2½ pounds beef chuck, cut into ½" cubes, patted dry with a paper
    towel
2–4 tablespoons olive oil
1 tablespoon brown sugar
2 tablespoons ground cumin
2 Spanish onions, coarsely chopped
4 cloves garlic, pressed or finely chopped
2 tablespoons peeled, finely chopped fresh gingerroot
1 orange or tangerine, peeled, seeded, and coarsely chopped
1 28-ounce can whole tomatoes, coarsely chopped

1. Mix flour and curry powder together and coat beef cubes.
Shake off excess.

2. Heat oil in a large soup pot until it is very hot (a drop of
water placed on the pan should sizzle). Cook beef cubes in small
batches, until browned on all sides. Set aside.

3. Add brown sugar, cumin, onions, and garlic to the pot and
sauté until onions have started to caramelize. (You may need to
add extra oil at this point.)

4. Stir in beef and remaining ingredients. Cook over low heat
until beef is tender, about 2 to 3 hours.

Curried Chicken Stew

4 tablespoons olive or safflower oil
2 Spanish onions, coarsely chopped
3 garlic cloves, pressed or finely chopped
4 1-pound cans Italian plum tomatoes, coarsely chopped
2–3 cups mango or apple chutney
3 Granny Smith apples, cored, peeled, and diced
2–3 cups chicken stock
⅓ cup all-purpose white flour
⅓ cup curry powder
3 pounds boneless, skinless chicken breasts, cut into serving sizes
Chopped fresh cilantro
Crème fraîche

1.   Heat 2 tablespoons oil over low flame in a heavy-bottomed pot. Add onions and garlic and cook, covered, until golden, 10 to 15 minutes.

2.   Add tomatoes, chutney, and apples; cook over medium heat for 20 minutes.

3.   Add chicken stock and cook for 1 hour.

4.   Mix flour and curry powder together and coat chicken pieces in this mixture; shake off excess.

5.   Heat remaining 2 tablespoons oil in a frying pan and brown chicken.

6.   When all the chicken has browned, set aside and add small amount of chicken stock to pan, scraping bottom. Pour into pot. Add chicken to pot and cook over low heat for 15 minutes.

7.   Garnish with fresh cilantro and crème fraîche.

This is a quick and easy stew, the perfect dish to serve for unexpected company. It tastes as if you've been slaving over a hot stove all day. Serve it with rice and a green salad.

SALLY NIRENBERG

Rosemary Chicken Stew

4 tablespoons olive or safflower oil
1 large Spanish onion, coarsely chopped
1 shallot, finely chopped
6 cloves garlic, pressed or finely chopped
2 oranges, peeled, seeded, and thinly sliced
1 16-ounce can whole peeled tomatoes, coarsely chopped
1 tablespoon crushed dried rosemary, or 3 tablespoons fresh
¼ teaspoon dried thyme, or ¾ teaspoon fresh
6 cups chicken stock
2 pounds skinless, boneless chicken breasts
2 tablespoons unsalted butter
3 cups chopped broccoli florets
¼ cup chopped fresh parsley
Salt and pepper

1.   Heat 2 tablespoons oil over low flame in a heavy-bottomed stewpot. Add onion, shallot, and garlic and cook until golden, about 15 minutes.

2.   Add oranges, tomatoes, rosemary, and thyme and sauté for 15 minutes.

3.   Add chicken stock and bring to a boil. Reduce heat to low and cook, partially covered, for 1 hour.

4.   Cut chicken breasts into bite-size pieces. Melt butter and remaining 2 tablespoons oil over high heat in a frying pan and brown chicken.

5.   When chicken has browned, set aside. Add small amount of stock from pot, scraping bottom of pan. Add to stewpot.

6.   Cover broccoli with boiling water and let sit for 5 minutes. Drain. Add broccoli, chicken, and parsley to stew; stir and cook over low heat for 5 minutes. Season with salt and pepper

7.   Serve immediately. (If you want to make this ahead of time, do not add broccoli until just prior to serving.)

Chilled Soups

In the not so distant past, only a few soups were considered appropriate for chilling, such as Gazpacho and Vichyssoise. However, it is now acceptable to chill almost anything, depending on your taste. I have one customer who eats her chili chilled and another who heats up Gazpacho!

The recipes in this chapter are always served chilled in my shop. However, these hot soups are also delicious chilled:

Asparagus with Tarragon
Broccoli with Dill
Carrot with Fennel
Carrot with Ginger Cream
Corn with Basil
Five Pepper
Parsnip with Sour Cream and
   Mustard

Tomato with Goat Cheese
Triple Tomato
Creamy Vegetable
Curried Zucchini with Cream
Zucchini Potato

The following chilled soups may also be served hot. Simply serve them as soon as preparation is completed. They may be reheated *gently;* do not let them boil.

Fresh Pea with Curry and
   Cream
Senegalese

Spinach with Garlic, Lemon,
   and Yogurt
Vichyssoise

Breakfast Fruit Soup

2 Granny Smith apples, unpeeled, cut up
3 bananas, sliced
1½ cups plain yogurt
2 cups fresh orange juice
½ teaspoon ground nutmeg
2 tablespoons chopped walnuts

1. Place apples in a food processor or blender and pulse until coarse.

2. Add remaining ingredients and process until smooth.

NOTE: You can substitute almost any fruit for the apples and bananas and almost any juice for the orange juice, but I have found this combination to be the best.

Technically, this isn't a soup at all, but since it's "souplike" and one of my favorite foods, I've included it. It is filling and wonderfully nutritious.

Cantaloupe and Honeydew with Ginger

This is
wonderfully
refreshing,
perfect for lunch
or dinner on a
hot summer day
when appetites
are flagging.

1 cantaloupe, peeled, seeded, and chopped
1 honeydew melon, peeled, seeded, and chopped
1½ cups plain yogurt
1½ tablespoons peeled, finely chopped fresh gingerroot
¼ teaspoon ground cinnamon
¼ cup walnuts

1.   Place all ingredients in a food processor, and process until smooth.

2.   Chill for at least 1 hour.

Cucumber Tomato

¼ cup lemon juice
1 46-ounce can tomato juice
2 tablespoons corn or safflower oil
1½ tablespoons curry powder
½ cup chopped fresh parsley
¼ cup red wine vinegar
1 cup buttermilk
2 cups plain yogurt
2 cucumbers, peeled, seeded, and finely sliced

1. Place all ingredients except cucumbers in a food processor or blender. Process until smooth.

2. Stir in cucumbers. Chill for 2 hours.

A cold soup from the Mediterranean.

Cucumber Walnut

Of Middle Eastern inspiration; try it before a dinner of broiled chicken or lamb.

1 cup coarsely chopped walnuts
2 cups plain yogurt
2 cups buttermilk
1 teaspoon salt
1 teaspoon black pepper
2 cloves garlic, pressed or finely chopped
2 cucumbers, peeled and coarsely chopped

1. Place all ingredients except cucumbers in a food processor and process until smooth.

2. Stir in chopped cucumbers and chill for 2 hours.

GAZPACHO

Gazpacho is a "liquid salad" and, generally, when people speak of gazpacho they mean the classic red gazpacho: tomatoes, cucumbers, peppers. In fact, for the first five years that I was in business, it was the only gazpacho I made. Don't be as hesitant as I was. The others are not just interesting, they are intriguing and refreshing.

Avocado Gazpacho

Somewhat like Red Gazpacho, somewhat like guacamole, and somewhat like salsa, this soup will heat you up and cool you down.

1 cucumber, peeled and chopped or thinly sliced
1 clove garlic, pressed or finely chopped
2 shallots, finely chopped
1 green or red pepper, cored, seeded, and chopped
2–3 tablespoons chopped fresh cilantro leaves
2 avocadoes, pitted, peeled, and chopped
1 tablespoon red wine vinegar
¼ teaspoon crushed red pepper flakes
2 tomatoes, diced
Juice of ½ lime
2 cups water

1.   Combine all ingredients.

2.   Remove half the solids and place in a food processor. Process briefly. Do not use a blender; this soup should have a chunky texture.

3.   Combine with remaining soup and chill for 1 hour.

Green Gazpacho

1 small onion, finely chopped
1 green pepper, cored, seeded, and diced
1 cucumber, peeled, seeded, and diced
2 garlic cloves, pressed or finely chopped
1 orange, peeled, pitted, and finely chopped
¼ cup chopped fresh cilantro leaves
2 cups ice water
1 teaspoon salt, or more to taste

Don't even think of making this without fresh cilantro.

1. Combine all ingredients.

2. Remove half the solids and place in a food processor. Do not use a blender. Pulse briefly and blend into remaining soup. Chill for 2 hours.

SALLY NIRENBERG

Orange Gazpacho

The orange juice and yellow pepper add just a touch of intriguing sweetness.

1 small red onion, finely chopped
1 tomato, diced
1 yellow pepper, cored, seeded, and chopped
1 cucumber, peeled, seeded, and diced
½ cup tomato juice
½ cup orange juice
Salt to taste

1.   Combine all ingredients.

2.   Remove half the solids and place in a food processor. Do not use a blender. Pulse briefly and blend into remaining soup. Chill for 2 hours.

Red Gazpacho

2 cucumbers, peeled and thinly sliced
2 tomatoes, diced
1 Spanish onion, coarsely chopped
2 red peppers, cored, seeded, and coarsely chopped
¼ cup olive oil
1 cup red wine vinegar
3 cups tomato juice
⅓ cup chopped fresh dill
2 teaspoons cayenne
1 teaspoon black pepper
1 teaspoon salt
1 cup ice water
Croutons

My version of the classic recipe.

1. Chop the first 4 ingredients, either by hand or by pulsing in a food processor. Do not use a blender.

2. Blend remaining ingredients except croutons and add to vegetables.

3. Chill for 2 hours. Garnish each serving with croutons.

White Gazpacho

While it's not entirely accurate to call this white, it is white-ish and of all gazpachos, the most unusual and absolutely my favorite. One bite gives you the sweetness of an apple, the next the zing of a scallion. It is the perfect summer refresher.

¾–1 cup small seedless green grapes
2 tablespoons chopped fresh dill
1 cucumber, peeled and chopped
1 Granny Smith apple, peeled, cored, and chopped
2–3 scallions (white and green parts), sliced
1½ cups plain yogurt or buttermilk
1½ cups ice water
Salt and pepper to taste
4 radishes, sliced paper thin

1.   Combine all ingredients except radishes.

2.   Remove half the solids and place in a food processor. Do not use a blender. Pulse briefly and stir into remaining soup. Chill for 2 hours.

3.   Garnish each serving with sliced radishes.

Fresh Pea with Curry and Cream

2 tablespoons unsalted butter
1 Spanish onion, coarsely chopped
2 teaspoons curry powder
1¼–1½ pounds fresh or frozen peas
5 cups water or chicken stock
½ cup heavy cream
½ teaspoon ground nutmeg

Suave and subtle, this is a great beginning for an elegant dinner.

1.   Melt butter over low heat in a medium saucepan. Add onion and cook, covered, until golden, about 15 minutes.

2.   Add curry powder, peas, and stock and bring to a boil. Reduce heat to low and cook for 35 to 45 minutes.

3.   Place solids in a food processor or blender. Process until smooth, gradually blending in remaining broth, heavy cream, and nutmeg. Chill for 2 hours.

SALLY NIRENBERG

Raspberry Lime

This refreshing soup ping-pongs in your mouth; it is, at once, tart, peppery, and sweet. Serve it as a first course, followed by either grilled chicken or grilled marinated flank steak.

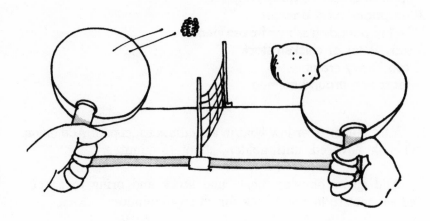

3 pints fresh raspberries, or 2 12-ounce packages frozen no sugar added, thawed
4 cups buttermilk
1 cup fresh orange juice
½ cup ice water
½ cup Triple Sec
Juice of 1 lime
½ teaspoon freshly grated nutmeg

1.   Place all ingredients in a food processor or blender. Process until smooth.

2.   Strain the mixture (if raspberry seeds bother you) and chill for 2 hours.

Senegalese

**YIELD
APPROXIMATELY
12 CUPS**

A luscious, flavorful, and mildly exotic blend of flavors.

2 tablespoons unsalted butter
1 bunch scallions, including greens, thinly sliced
½ cup grated unsweetened fresh or dried coconut
1 carrot, peeled and sliced
1 stalk celery, sliced
3 tablespoons curry powder
8 cups chicken stock
¾ pound skinless, boneless chicken breast
2 cups heavy cream
2 oranges, peeled, pits removed

1.   Melt butter over medium heat in a large saucepan or soup pot. Add scallions and coconut and cook, covered, until they begin to brown, about 10 minutes.

2.   Add carrot, celery, and curry powder and cook for an additional 5 minutes.

3.   Add chicken stock and bring to a boil. Reduce heat to low and cook until vegetables are tender, about 5 minutes.

4.   Add chicken and cook until tender, about 10 minutes. Remove chicken and set aside.

5.   Place solids in a food processor. Process until very smooth, gradually adding remaining broth and heavy cream.

6.   Coarsely chop chicken and oranges and blend into soup. Chill for 2 hours.

NOTE: Do not substitute light cream for the heavy cream. This soup must be rich.

Spinach with Garlic, Lemon, and Yogurt

The idea for this soup came from Laura Putney, who worked at the Brookline Place store. When Laura first came to work, she tried just about every soup, and almost without fail would tell me that it was the best whatever-it-was that she had ever had. It got to be a joke, because while she actually said it as if she meant it, I told her that I'd pay no attention to her judgment: she seemed to love everything. This combination of flavors was her idea, and while she ate the soup, I ate my words.

2 tablespoons olive oil
8 garlic cloves, pressed or finely chopped
1 10-ounce bag spinach, thoroughly washed and coarsely chopped, or 1 package chopped frozen, thawed and drained
4 cups chicken stock
2 tablespoons fresh lemon juice
½ cup plain yogurt
Freshly ground black pepper to taste

1. Heat oil over low flame in a heavy-bottomed saucepan. Add garlic and cook, covered, until golden, about 15 minutes.

2. Add chopped spinach and sauté for 10 minutes.

3. Add chicken stock and bring to a boil. Reduce heat to low and cook for 10 minutes.

4. Chill for 2 hours.

5. Place solids in a food processor or blender. Process until smooth, gradually adding remaining broth, lemon juice, yogurt, and pepper.

VARIATION:

If you want a richer soup, substitute cream or sour cream for the yogurt.

Vichyssoise

1 bunch leeks, sliced (3½–4 cups)
¼ cup unsalted butter
4 medium red bliss potatoes, unpeeled, cubed (3½–4 cups)
5 cups chicken stock
¾ cup heavy cream, or ½ cup heavy cream and ¼ cup sour cream
½ teaspoon ground nutmeg
¼ teaspoon black pepper

The classic. It shouldn't be toyed with. Though the traditional recipe calls for peeled potatoes, I keep the skins on; they add texture and flecks of color.

1.   Cut off root end and 3 inches of green part of leeks and discard. Quarter leeks lengthwise and thinly slice. Soak them in several changes of water, being careful to get rid of all the sand.

2.   Melt butter in a large heavy-bottomed saucepan. Add leeks and cook, covered, until wilted, about 15 minutes.

3.   Add potatoes and chicken stock. Cover and bring to a boil. Reduce heat to low and cook, uncovered, until potatoes are tender, about 20 minutes.

4.   Place solids in a food processor. Process until completely smooth, gradually adding remaining broth.

5.   Blend in cream, nutmeg, and pepper. Chill for 2 hours.